The Abraham Lincoln of the Sea

The Abraham Lincoln of the Sea

The Life of Andrew Furuseth

Arnold Berwick

Odin Press
Santa Cruz

FIRST EDITION

Library of Congress Number: 92–64186

ISBN: 0–9633611–0–4

93 94 95 96 97—10 9 8 7 6 5 4 3 2 1

Printed in Singapore.

Design and composition by Detta Penna, Design + Production

"You can put me in jail, but you cannot give me narrower quarters than as a seaman I have always had. You cannot give me coarser food than I have always eaten. You cannot make me any lonelier than I have always been."

Andrew Furuseth

Acknowledgments

I am grateful to Karl Kortum, Curator and Founder of the San Francisco Maritime National Historical Park, for his generous help in the research and the editing of this book. Also thanks to John Bircheff for his contribution, and to Detta Penna for her design work and for her wholehearted support.

Preface

In 1934, I was a 14-year-old boy when I went to St. Luke's Hospital in San Francisco to see my father, who had been badly injured in an accident. He said to me, "Across the hall . . . a good Norwegian . . . name is Andrew Furuseth."

I went across the hall, peeked into the room, and saw an old white-haired man who was propped up in bed and fast asleep. But I was concerned about my father who was near death, so I didn't think much more about Andrew Furuseth at that time.

It is only now that I realize I had been privileged to stand in the presence of a great and noble spirit, in the presence of a man who yearned and fought to secure freedom and justice for others. Time after time, he was beaten down, only to rise again. And all the while he unselfishly refused any gain for himself. He was a leader unlike any we have today.

It is refreshing and comforting to know that honest leaders existed—and, hopefully, exist. Such men should not be forgotten.

The Abraham Lincoln of the Sea

Chapter One

A boy stood alone in the middle of the road, staring at the driver of a horse and wagon as he drew away. The boy listened intently to the clip-clops of the horse's hooves and to the sound of the squeaky wheels he knew so well—and wondered if he would ever hear those sounds again. As the wagon approached a bend in the road, the driver, the boy's father, raised his arm in a final farewell, and disappeared behind a row of birch trees.

With a look of resignation in his hazel eyes, the boy pressed his lips together tightly, as though to suppress any outward appearance of what he felt more deeply inside. His eyes squinted slightly, transforming his countenance to one of strong determination—a characteristic that would dominate his life.

His name was Anders Andreassen Furuseth: Anders, who was the son of Andreas, and who was born in a place called Furuseth, in Romedal, about 50 miles north of present-day Oslo, in Norway.

He stood for some time, thinking. He knew it was only right that he leave home, and that he never go back there to live. He knew his father's skimpy wages as caretaker of a dam at Damstua was not enough to support a family of ten children. One should be grateful to be able to eat fish, potatoes, and bread made of flour mixed with bark of the elm tree. But even these had been scarce during the past hard winter. Yes, it was only right that he leave home, that he come to the Schjotz farm at Ostby to work for his keep. It was time he made his own way. After all, he was no longer a child . . . He was eight years old.

In that year of 1862, great events were taking place in faraway America. President Abraham Lincoln, after many battles in the Civil War, would save the Union and free black slaves.

Who could have foretold that Anders would also fight many battles, would also save a union (the sailors' union), and would also free slaves (American seamen who were held in bondage)? Who could have foreseen that this young Norwegian boy would someday be called the "Abraham Lincoln of the Sea"?

T HE YEAR 1862 was one of the hardest of times in Norway. Outside of fishing, about the only way to make a living was in farming, and the stony land had always been stingy in yielding enough to eat. To make matters worse, as the population of Norway continued to increase, the struggle for food became even more intense. People were hungry. Discord and conflict became common. There was much suffering.

Anders's move to the farm of Jonas S. Schjotz proved to be a fortunate one. For one thing, although he had to work hard as a farmhand, he ate regularly. But, something far more important occurred: He met the parish clerk, a man named Hansen.

In those days there was no regular school attendance for common people. There were only private schools, those connected to the church. Hansen was in charge of the one at Rohne. He saw that Anders had a keen and inquisitive mind, and an unusual interest in learning. He took the boy in and guided him in his studies. He stressed the teachings of the Bible, and imbued Anders with a deep sense of right and wrong, of obligations, of justice—lessons which Anders absorbed so completely that they became an inflexible and permanent part of him. They shaped the man he was to become.

By the time Anders was confirmed in 1869, he had a fairly good education, but he was eager to learn more. He continued to study foreign languages, history, anything he could lay his hands on. He was a lifetime student of the Bible.

At the age of 19, the sea and the search for adventure tempted him. In 1873, he stepped on board the bark *Marie* out of Drammen, and set sail to see the world he had been reading and dreaming about.

Because Furuseth spoke so little about himself in later years, we don't know much about his seafaring days. He seemed so familiar with ports throughout the world that he must have sailed most of the seven seas. He sailed in ships under many flags, but seemed especially attracted to the American. He truly believed in what he regarded as the greatest political document ever written, particularly the lines proclaiming that "all men are created equal." He wanted to see the country that produced such a profound belief.

In the first half of the 19th century, American ships were well-built and well-manned. Sons of the best families went to sea with the view of advancing upward. The Yankee sailors were neatly dressed and knew their trade well. Officers started their careers with training in mathematics, navigation, and ship's husbandry. Captains, who usually were part owners of their vessels, could afford to live as gentlemen, and were treated as such when ashore. The Yankee ship and her crew were the pride of the ocean.

Around the middle of the century, the nation's interest turned inland. There was a wide expanse of land to settle, factories to be established, and railroads to be built. The cowboy, not the sailor, was soon to become the national symbolic hero. Young, aggressive Americans turned their backs on the sea, so the shipowners had to look to foreigners to man their ships.

At that time, economic conditions in Europe were at their worst, especially in Scandinavia. Norwegians, Swedes, Danes, and Finns, unable to eke out a living at home, fled to America. Most were attracted by free farm land in the American West, and some came as sailors.

Now that common foreigners manned the ships, the shipowners no longer found it necessary to maintain the living standards of earlier days. At the time Furuseth went to sea, when a sailor boarded a ship he brought all his possessions with him in a sea chest or perhaps just a canvas sea bag: a simple mess kit, work pants and shirts, oilskins, sheath knife, and sea boots.

His quarters were in a black, ill-ventilated, poorly-lighted hole called a forecastle, which was often damp and soggy because of water dripping from leaks in the upper deck. His bed was a hard board bunk, rarely more than five feet long. If he wanted a little comfort, he had to furnish and bring with him a bit of straw stuffed into a cheap mattress cover (called "a donkey's breakfast").

Being without refrigeration, the normal fare for the seaman was salt beef or salt pork (both of which came in casks of brine which usually stank when opened), pea soup, porridge, and biscuits and bread (often infested with weevils, dead and harmless from baking and completely ignored in time).

In the 1870s, many of the ships had no sheltered eating place for the crew. As a rule, their quarters, the forecastle, had headroom of no more than four and a half or five feet, and was jam-packed with bunks. So the sailors had to eat out on the deck. The cook would bring out a pot, and the men had to hunker around the pot on the deck while they ate, regardless of rain, wind, snow, or spray of the sea. If the spray hit the hard salty side of pork or the salty tough cow's meat, it really didn't matter because both were already so salty that a little sea water didn't make any difference. It was worse when the spray got into the pea soup because it made the soup even thinner and saltier. It was still worse when the spray got into the porridge pot, because the sea water made the porridge almost impossible to eat.

Often soaked with rain and spray, and without a change of clothes, the sailor might become a victim of rheumatism. Poor food brought on scurvy. Sailors suffered from tuberculosis because of the foul, stifling air in the forecastle. Young men, some still in their thirties, often became diseased, and were cast aside and left to die a lonely and lingering death.

To many, death came more quickly through wrecks and drownings. Heavy, stormy weather was not the only cause for this loss of lives. Ships were run for a profit, so the temptation to overload the cargo existed. An overloaded vessel might sail safely for a time; with good luck, for a long time. But when encountering exceptionally heavy weather, she might not be able to withstand the pounding, and she might go to the bottom—because of what is blasphemously called "an act of God." The shipowner suffered no loss because he was insured—or over-insured—but "poor Jack" lost his life.

At the time Furuseth sailed, as many of the oldest and worst wooden vessels were lost or scrapped, they were replaced by steamships. The number of deaths by drowning in wrecks decreased as the use of sailing ships declined, but the number of deaths from disease in steamships rose. Tuberculosis was the largest single killer disease.

An able-bodied seaman was expected to be physically strong and agile, and to be able to perform a variety of skills. He had to know the use of every part of the standing and running rigging of the vessel; know various knots and splices; know the use of rigging screws, marlin spikes, serving mallets, and all the shipboard tools. He had to take his turn at the wheel, and to be able to steer the ship under all conditions, in all kinds of currents, and in foul weather as well as fair. Anchors must be secured, hatches battened down, lines coiled and put away. The able seamen needed agility to climb up the rigging and to work in places where both handhold and foothold were precarious. ("One hand for the owner and one for yourself.") When no other work was immediately necessary, there was always chipping of rust, scraping, and painting to be done.

When Furuseth learned his trade and became an able-bodied seaman, he received wages of 18 dollars a month.

Although a seaman's daily tasks may have been no harder or easier than those of workers on land, there were important differences in his situation. For one thing, his ship was not just a place to work; it was his home. His shipmates were not merely fellow employees, but his social companions whom he lived with night and day, day after day, month after month. A voyage from New York to San Francisco around the Cape took four to six months.

Even more important was the difference in standing

between the boss of the worker on land and the master of a ship. If a worker on land was discontented with his boss or his work, he could go on strike, or he could quit his job and go elsewhere. He was free to do as he wished.

Not so the sailor.

When a sailor wanted to get a job on a ship, he had to sign Articles of Agreement, a contract between him and the vessel. The articles set forth the name of the ship, the prospective voyage, the sailor's rating, the rate of wages, and the time of termination of the contract. The sailor had no choice. If he wanted to work, he had to sign the articles. And once he signed them he was bound to the ship for the duration of the voyage. He was no longer a free man. He belonged to the ship until the contract expired.

A workman ashore could protest his grievances by stopping work, and he was deemed a "striker." If a seaman stopped work and left the ship while under contract, he was declared a "deserter." Desertion was a criminal act. Far back in history, the crime was punishable by branding on the forehead with a red hot iron. In later days, desertion remained a crime but the punishment was changed. In 1790, the new government of the United States enacted legislation providing for the arrest, imprisonment, and the return to their ship of "deserting" sailors. The 1872 Shipping Commissioner's Act reinforced this rule. The sailors were considered "wards of admiralty," under the care of their guardian, the state.

So, regardless of what grievances a sailor might have, he could not leave the ship until the voyage ended. He was a virtual slave. And he had plenty of reasons for wanting to leave. In addition to poor food, cramped quarters, bad working conditions, and low pay, the seaman sometimes suffered the brutality of the "buckoes."

By a law of 1835, beating, wounding, or almost any kind of physical punishment by a captain or mate, was prohibited . . . "if without justifiable cause." Unfortunately, the law courts and juries consistently found that the assaults upon seamen were "justifiable." Flogging was abolished by federal statute in 1850, but all other forms of punishment remained. The captain usually turned the dirty work over to one of his mates, some of whom got a reputation as a "bucko."

In many cases it was found that members of the crew were knocked down, kicked, and beaten with rope ends and even with iron belaying pins. Arms and legs were broken, and ribs were stomped in by heavy sea boots. During Furuseth's sailing days, one form of torture was that known as "tricing up," which consisted of ironing a man by the wrists, passing a rope around the irons, and hoisting him up until his toes barely touched the deck. He might be tortured in this way for six, eight, and ten hours, sometimes resulting in dislocated and paralyzed arms.

Furuseth witnessed these deeds of the buckoes. On one ship, the second mate beat a seaman so badly that one of his eyes was nearly put out, and his mouth was so badly injured that he could scarcely eat or sleep. A few days later, the first mate broke a sailor's nose and disfigured him with brass knuckles. Another seaman was so cruelly treated that he jumped overboard and committed suicide. Four other members of the crew were mistreated. This all occurred on one ship during one voyage.

And if a sailor tried to leave the ship to escape this treatment, he was guilty of the crime of desertion. He could be arrested, imprisoned, and brought back to his ship. It is easy to imagine what further treatment he might then expect at the hands of a bucko.

Sometimes a victim sought relief in the courts, but time after time the verdict was "justifiable cause."

Even if the law had been more favorable to the victim, it would have been difficult for the sailor to get justice. To protect a brutal mate, the captain would send him ashore before the ship dropped anchor and before the sailor could leave the ship and get to the authorities. Later, the mate would quietly return when the ship was ready to depart for the next voyage. And it did no good to complain against the captain. He had merely to have a bill of exceptions prepared, file a bond, and sail away, leaving the poor seaman, without money or work, to wait a few months until the court could hear his case—which he had no chance of winning anyway because his only witnesses, his shipmates, had shipped out or drifted off.

This was the situation that existed on board some ships when Anders (who now became known as Andrew) appeared on the scene. He was tall, broad-shouldered, muscular, and capable of handling himself in any contest of strength. And yet, he already exhibited some of the characteristics that marked him in later life as a recluse, devoted to reading and meditation. He had developed the hardened body of a working sailor, but he had the mind of a philosopher. His eyes had a contemplative look; he was always observing, thinking.

"I saw men abused," he once said, "beaten into insensibility. I saw sailors try to escape from brutal masters, and from unseaworthy vessels upon which they had been lured to serve. I saw them hunted down and thrown into the ship's hold in chains. I saw the bitterness of it all from experience."

He had an experience of his own which profoundly altered the course of his life. He was stricken with a fever while sailing on the Indian Ocean. He lay in an upper bunk in the filthy, crowded forecastle, perspiring and feeling weak. An unmerciful first mate dragged him out of the bunk and forced him on deck to carry out his normal duties. When his watch ended, Furuseth crawled back up into his bunk, determined not to "turn to" again until he was feeling better. As his temperature rose, his anger rose with it. He lay facing shipside with a sharp knife clasped in his hand, mentally rehearsing his movements when the mate should again lay hands on him. A sudden twist of the body, and a plunge of the knife into the mate's throat. He would *kill* the mate.

Hours passed, and then days. The mate didn't return. After a long period of delirium, Furuseth recovered and went back on deck.

Then a reaction set in. He might have *killed* a man! What would his parents think? How ashamed they would be to hear the news that their son had killed a mate, that he had been hanged to the yardarm for murder. He agonized over the thought while in his bunk, and repented during long wheel watches. Why, he pondered, should this have happened to him? What had almost caused him to be a murderer?

His thoughts turned to the teachings of Parish Clerk Hansen. He had taught justice, fair treatment, concern for others. The ship's officers violated all these civilized rules. They were cruel and brutal in their treatment of the sailors.

Furuseth feared no man, and knew that, if it need be, he could handle himself one-on-one in any fair fight. But it was futile to fight back. The captain was master of the ship, was the law onto himself. As long as the sailor stayed onboard, he was powerless to resist. And if he left the ship, he was branded a criminal. The sailor was in a hopeless position.

Furuseth finally concluded that the situation could be corrected only if the sailor could leave his ship if he chose to. Other workers could quit their work, but not the sailor. He was bound to his ship. He was a slave. Whatever happened to the proclamation that "all men are created equal"? The sailors were not equal. They were slaves.

The sailor must be set free . . . must be set *free*.

Surely, something could be done to help "poor Jack."

But, what?

Chapter Two

San Francisco had a humble beginning, on land once officially described as "uninhabitable." Bounded by the Pacific Ocean on the west, an inland bay on the east, and a narrow strait connecting the two, the peninsula had seven hills and a wasteland of sand, relieved only by some clumps of sagebrush, stunted oaks, and a few jack rabbits and coyotes. On the bay side of the peninsula, Yerba Buena Cove extended inland. The cove was shallow, and at low tide became a mud flat.

In 1835, Captain William Richardson erected San Francisco's first dwelling—a tent made of four redwood posts and a ship's foresail. The following year, he built a shanty of rough boards on the shore of the cove. He traded in hides and tallow, which he gathered from around the bay shores and from up the rivers, and delivered to the ships which occasionally sailed into the harbor. Later, he replaced his shanty with a two-story adobe building that stood for many years.

Other traders arrived, followed by settlers. Homes were built. Vioget's combination restaurant, billiard room, and saloon became the most important of the buildings in the new village of Yerba Buena. More people came. Ten years after Richardson settled on the land, California was taken from Mexico by the United States as a consequence of the Mexican War, and the name of the entire tip of the peninsula was changed from Yerba Buena to San Francisco in 1847.

By this year, many of the town's 850 citizens, who

believed that the tide flats would eventually be filled in and built over, had purchased "water lots" (under water at high tide) at 50 to 100 dollars each, at locations under today's financial district. William S. Clark built the first wharf at what is now the foot of Broadway. No longer would it be necessary to move barrels and boxes by lighter from the ship to the beach or to land through sticky mud. However, Clark's wharf could handle only one ship at a time. The brig *Belfast* was the first seagoing vessel to "come alongside" in San Francisco.

In 1848, the town had a few warehouses, more shanties, two hotels, a church, and several saloons. New settlers continued to arrive in ships or in covered wagons, and citizens looked forward to a slow but steady growth.

Then gold was discovered on the American River.

News of the discovery spread, and ships from all over the world converged on California. New arrivals dropped their anchors in the cove, and the crew—mates as well as seamen— were often over the side even before the passengers could disembark. All rushed to the diggings. A few returned to San Francisco with fortunes in their belts. Business flourished. Gambling dens sprang up, soon to become the Barbary Coast with its booze, prostitutes, drugs, and a nefarious reputation.

More and more ships sailed into the cove, but not all left. As stated, for the most part they were deserted by their crews. Some of the idle vessels were used as warehouses, stores, hotels, and offices. The first bank in San Francisco was a scow beached at California and Battery Streets, now the heart of today's financial district, but then the shoreline of the bay. But many of the ships were abandoned. By July of '49, more than 200 craft lay idle in the cove. Since there never was a wooden ship built that didn't leak (according to Furuseth), and since there was no crew on board to man the pumps, some of the ships gradually sank into the mud or at their moorings.

Piles were driven into the mud flats to construct more wharves, each backed by a group of merchants trying to get nearer the deep water offshore. As more wharves were built, they were connected crosswise by a network of "running bridges," consisting of narrow platforms of planks, a few feet wide.

Some people preferred to live across the bay in Contra Costa (Spanish for the "opposite coast" or "shore"). The July 17, 1852 issue of the *Daily Alta California* newspaper carried an ad of the Contra Costa Ferry Company: "On and after this date the steam ferryboat *E. Corning,* with Captain B. H. Ramsdell, will make four crossings between San Francisco and Contra Costa . . . Her cabins are elegantly furnished . . . fitted at great expense expressly for this ferry route, and possesses every convenience for the ferriage of passengers, freight, stock, and wagons."

San Franciscans began to fill in some of the "water lots," beginning with that area that extended eastward from Montgomery to Davis Streets and southward from Battery to Market. Blasting the side of Telegraph Hill produced tens of thousands of cubic yards of sandstone and shale. Dozens of horse-drawn carts hauled the freshly blasted rock to be dumped on the shoreline of the cove. Sand for bay fill came from the city's seemingly inexhaustible dunes. Slowly, the shoreline of Yerba Buena Cove pushed farther eastward, creeping across the mud at the rate of about one block a year. In its path lay the hulks of sunken ships, in some cases only their masts protruding above water. The fill moved on, burying ships and rotting piers, always requiring the wharves to be extended even farther and farther into the bay water.

A planked street was constructed on the pilings, parallel to the shoreline. Called East Street, it took off in many directions, threading through the wharves. In some places it ran straight, at many points it discontinued, then sprang up suddenly for a stretch. As the city changed shape, so did East Street, but always it remained the waterfront, the bay side boundary of San Francisco. (Since 1909, East Street has been called the Embarcadero.)

The tides ate away at the landfill, occasionally causing a building to totter or an unsteady wharf to collapse. Temporary seawalls, or bulkheads, were built. In 1878 began the construction of a permanent seawall, constructed of heavy rock backed with sand fill inshore. (Construction was started near present-day Fisherman's Wharf and moved southward to China Basin, section by section, until it was substantially completed in 1914.)

W hen a ship came in from the Pacific, through the Golden Gate, and into San Francisco Bay, the sailors' spirits were always high. They yearned for a soft bed, good food, whiskey, a woman, maybe even a good cigar. They knew they would soon be in the hands of a runner, the person who would quickly furnish them with all their desires.

This arrival into the port of San Francisco can best be described by the 1876 first-hand account of Frederick Perry, mate on the *Continental*, as quoted in *Fair Winds & Foul:*—

"We soon rounded Fort Point, opening up the Presidio on our right, and then headed over for our anchoring ground off Alcatraz Island . . . All fore and aft sails were now quickly hauled down, unbent and stowed away in lockers. On the signal from the tug we let go our anchor and once more were tied fast to mother earth. A fleet of small boats quickly surrounded us, manned by a loud-mouthed lot of boardinghouse runners, who swooped down like birds of prey, quickly to befog the brains of our crew by feeding them with a vile concoction of whisky that soon produced a half-drunken stupor, in which condition they were taken ashore and were soon robbed of the few hard-earned dollars they might have coming to them . . .

"It was one of the strict rules of the ship that no runners should be allowed on deck until all the work was finished and the crew dismissed, but it took a strong man armed with a heavy oak heaver to keep the more persistent ones from clambering over the side. When held in check they threw small packages over the side of the ship containing bottles of their vile stuff and a couple of cigars with a printed card attached, setting forth in glowing terms the superior quality of the accommodation to be obtained at their particular house over that of their competitors, keeping up in the meantime a running line of talk that would put a ballyhoo man at a side show to shame.

"Calling in the most endearing terms to the men as they worked aloft or passed along the deck, they begged them in the name of all that is holy not to forget the Jackson's or Chandler's, as their respective home might have been designated, was next to the Garden of Eden—the nearest to a perfect Elysium for poor, tired, overworked sailors that could be found on earth. And the strange part of it was that, after being skinned or half flayed alive in every port they entered, darned if the poor fellows, with but few exceptions, didn't believe what they were told."

After describing the remaining chores of the sailors, Perry continues:

" . . . and the crew was dismissed. The hungry runners now sprang over the rails and made a grand rush for their victims like the lions in the Colosseum. Within fifteen minutes the last sailor and his dunnage had gone over the side and the fleet of runners' boats headed away towards the city front and 'Liberty'."

The sailor was welcomed at the boardinghouse with open arms. In Hyman Weintraub's *Andrew Furuseth, Emancipator of the Seamen*, we find the following:

"At the boardinghouse the sailor was provided with a bed, food and drink, cigars, and even clothes and supplies. If he ran out of money, the boardinghouse keeper extended credit; if he went on a binge, the keeper sobered him up; if he got into trouble with the police, the keeper had connections to 'spring him from the brig.' . . .

"For all these services the sailor paid dearly. When he came ashore, he was charged five dollars by the runner, a dollar for the boat, and another dollar for the wagon that took him to the house. There he paid five dollars per week whether he stayed one night or all week. He had to buy supplies for his next trip: five dollars for oils, some more for cigars, a tin plate, a pot, a bundle of matches, a plug of tobacco, and a straw bed. It was no secret that the sailor was overcharged for everything he bought . . . "

Why would the boardinghouse keeper be willing to give credit to a penniless sailor? Indeed, not only be willing but actually luring him in by the services of a runner.

It was part of an established economic arrangement under which a ship's captain, instead of hiring sailors individually, relied on a seamen's boardinghouse to round up his crew. A sailor could get a job on board ship only through the boardinghouse. If he didn't live there—and run up a large bill—he couldn't get a job. The boardinghouse keeper maintained his hold over the sailor by controlling his employment.

A key factor in the system was the right of the boarding-house to collect the wages of the seaman directly from the captain of his ship. The keeper collected any remaining wages earned by the sailor on the incoming voyage, and, by means of an advance or allotment note, he could collect part of the wages yet to be earned by the sailor on the outgoing voyage.

Also, if the seaman protested his indebtedness, or objected to shipping out as the keeper ordered him to, the law provided that his clothes could be held by the boardinghouse keeper for debt. This was an effective club over his head, because without money or clothes, the sailor couldn't go far.

So, a sailor soon learned that when he landed in port he might as well go along with the system—live it up until his credit ran out. If he didn't drink or squander his money, or if he actually tried to save a little nest egg, there were no jobs for him. The sooner he used up his credit at the boardinghouse, the faster he could return to the sea.

As if this situation wasn't bad enough, another creature entered the picture to further bleed the sailor. The "crimp" was a middleman, like an employment agent, who arranged with a captain to furnish the crew, and with a boardinghouse to find berths for its guests. The crimp charged each sailor five dollars for a "chance"—the fee of the employment agent. He hired and controlled the runners, collected the advances, and sometimes even collected commissions on everything the sailor spent while on shore. Although the boardinghouse keeper took advantage of the sailors, he did furnish what the sailors needed to have some fun on shore and to do as they pleased for a change. Also, the alternative to a sailor's boardinghouse was to easily fall prey to some city slicker in a waterfront bar and end up by losing his entire voyage pay, as well as losing the food, drink, and a job that the keeper provided. All in all, it might be worth it. But the sailors hated the crimp because from him they got nothing in return. He was a cunning leech.

Why would a man put up with this situation, and suffer the indignity of being in an inferior and degrading social position? Why didn't he leave the sea and live a normal life on land? Firstly, because most sailors actually liked their way of life. They took pride and satisfaction in learning seamanship, and in meeting the challenge of sea and wind. They enjoyed the life on sea and the occasional flings on land. Also, the average sailor was virtually penniless and was always in "debt," with no place to stay on land except the boardinghouse that enticed him in, and with no "home" except his ship. And booze helped to form his habits. He was locked into a system he could not escape.

In August of 1880, at the age of 26, Furuseth sailed into San Francisco Bay on a British vessel out of Calcutta. Runners swarmed over the deck, and Furuseth soon found himself in a rowboat with two shipmates, pulling up to a wharf on the San Francisco waterfront. The runner led them to a horse and wagon. The sailors tossed their seabags on the wagon and climbed on.

Fog rolled in, chilling the air.

After months of gazing at the open sea, Furuseth stared with intent interest at the sights that passed by: to his right, a ship chandler, with an anchor, blocks, chain, and wire rope spread out in front of his business establishment . . . a row of one- and two-story wooden frame buildings . . . boarding-house . . . saloon . . . restaurant . . . Chinese laundry . . . chop house . . . saloon . . . pawn broker . . . barber . . . saloon . . .

Now, to the left he saw a long one-story wooden building—the Ferry House—behind which were the slips for the dozens of ferryboats that plied the routes between San Francisco and the other bay cities. The building was covered with signs: Central Pacific Railroad . . . Enterprise Brewery Company . . . Pet Cigarettes . . . Days of '49 Whiskey . . . Pat Rooney Cigars . . .

He saw activity in front of the Ferry House. Wagons, carriages, and low-slung drays crisscrossed the broad section of East Street, their wheels clattering over the cobblestone roadway. Horse-drawn streetcars, with bells clanging, came down Market Street, made a turn, and headed up Market toward the distant Twin Peaks.

People moved about, some leisurely and some quickly with a fixed determination. A huge bell in the Ferry House tower clanged loudly, then clanged again. From out of nearby restaurants and saloons, others emerged and walked rapidly to catch the next ferryboat that was soon to leave.

The wagon in which Furuseth was riding turned up Market Street for one block, then turned south along Steuart Street for a short distance. It stopped in front of a boarding-house. This was to be Furuseth's home until he shipped out again. He was in the grip of the crimp.

In the morning, he looked out of the second-floor window of his room. The block across the street was narrow between Steuart and East Streets, but was long running from Market to Mission. There were buildings at the Market Street end, but the rest of the block was covered with open lumber yards and two hay barns. Beyond East Street and south of the Ferry House, wharves extended out into the bay: Mission Street Wharf, Howard Street Wharf, and Folsom Street Wharf. He saw the tall masts of sailing ships, a few with their bowsprits protruding over East Street.

Later in the day, Furuseth walked south along Steuart Street. On his right, he saw more frame buildings—some already dilapidated—housing a ship chandler, a boat shop, saloons, a restaurant, boarding and rooming houses. Empty whiskey bottles lay strewn about. As he crossed the Mission Street intersection and proceeded on to Howard, he noticed that although Steuart Street and the buildings on his right were built on solid ground, everything to his left—the lumberyards, the extension of Howard Street, and East Street itself—were built on pilings and planks over bay water.

When he saw a sign reading "Three Finger Jack's Saloon," he turned in. He found the place to be of the usual kind, with sawdust on the floor and a bar along one side of the room—handrail and footrail and plenty of large brass spittoons. Furuseth liked his whiskey, although he never drank to excess. And he liked the companionship of a sailors' saloon. Here he was among seafaring men who came in to do a little friendly drinking and talking. Although Furuseth could speak French, German, and English, he preferred to speak his native Norwegian. In Three Finger Jack's he met four of his countrymen who told him something about San Francisco, what to see, and what to watch out for. Furuseth asked if there was a library in town, but his drinking companions didn't know of any. So he set out in search. He walked up to Market Street and headed west.

Market Street, once a narrow path wavering between and over sand dunes, was now a wide, cobbled thoroughfare, stretching from the Ferry House out toward Twin Peaks. South of Market Street, the Mission District, the working-class section, was expanding rapidly to the south and west. To the north lay the produce area and the Barbary Coast near the waterfront, and the business district with offices, hotels, theaters, and shops.

Millionaires were more numerous here in San Francisco than in any other city in the country. The Big Four railroad barons and the silver Bonanza Kings had built mansions on top of Nob Hill, each larger and more grand than the next. Because the streets up Nob Hill were too steep and slippery for a horse, a man named Hallidie had invented a new means of transportation: a streetcar that was pulled up the hill by an underground cable.

Furuseth walked up Market Street in search of a library. Block after block, the street was lined with banks, hotels, theaters, and office buildings—most with facades covered with elaborate decorations of stone or cast iron. In answer to his query, a passer-by directed him to the Mechanics' Institute Library on Post Street, just off Market. Furuseth found the library, but noticed a small sign which advised that the facilities were for members only. "$1.00 initiation and $1.50 quarterly dues." With wages of 18 dollars a month, most of which went to his crimp, there was no hope of becoming a member here.

Informed of another library on Bush Street, he found the Mercantile Library, three stories high, an elegant structure with a reading room, smoking room, museum, ladies and gentlemen's dressing rooms. It boasted of 50,000 volumes of books, 116 magazines, and 25 illustrated papers. He was informed that membership required a "$2.00 initiation fee and $3.00 quarterly, paid in advance." So much for the Mercantile Library.

Furuseth finally located another library two blocks farther up on Bush Street. The year before, in 1879, the city had rented Pacific Hall and started a public library, a library that could be used by anyone—free. Furuseth went in and stayed until they led him to the door and turned off the lights. Here he found books on maritime law, history, Shakespeare, philosophy—all the treasures he craved but was denied on his long, insular voyages. And here they were, available to everyone, rich and poor alike.

He wandered around the city for a couple of days, and liked what he saw. He enjoyed music, but seldom had the chance to hear much except sea chanties and such. Here, the Dashaway Hall held concerts, and one could see *H.M.S. Pinafore* at the Bush Street Theater for two bits and Grand Opera at Tivoli Gardens for four bits. And the library was close at hand. He would like to stay in San Francisco for a while, but when his advance was used up, the crimp would ship him out on another long voyage. It would be many months, maybe years, before he could return to San Francisco.

But one night in the dining room of the boardinghouse, a fellow sailor told him that he was shipping out the next morning and would be back in about two weeks. Furuseth questioned him, then went to the public library to read newspapers, books, and reports. Characteristically, he studied the situation in depth, and soon realized that the history and unique conditions on the Pacific Coast offered a seaman opportunities he had never seen before.

He learned that in earlier days the sailors got occasional work carrying hides and tallow from California ranches. With the gold rush, commerce had expanded and flourished. It received a strong impetus from the completion of the transcontinental railroad in 1869. More people moved in. Vast fields of wheat were sown. The grain of California couldn't bear the high railway charge to the East, but it could afford the ocean rate around Cape Horn. To San Francisco came the largest and best sailing vessels of all the maritime nations of the world. People flooded in to take advantage of new opportunities.

With the rapid spread of settlements all along the Pacific Coast, the demand for lumber became insatiable. Hundreds of small mills were set up in the redwood forests of California and the Douglas fir forests of Washington and Oregon. There were as yet no railroads leading out of the forests, so a fleet of two-masted schooners was built to haul lumber to San Francisco and other coastal cities. They were later supplemented by three- and even four-masters, particularly for the northern mills in Oregon and Washington. At times, they couldn't bring lumber in fast enough to meet the needs.

In deep water voyages, it was customary for the sailors to bring a vessel into port and then spend a week or two on the beach. The cargo was discharged and loaded by longshoremen—"men along the shore." Furuseth knew from bitter experience that this provided the shipowners with another opportunity to victimize "poor Jack."

If the ship was to have a long layover in port, the captain would have to feed and pay a crew he really didn't need. Also, if through some oversight a sailor might still have some wages due him, it was to the captain's benefit to have the sailor "desert." It not only cut down on further expenses, but the law provided for the forfeiture of any past due wages. So, on some ships, before the vessel put into a harbor, the bucko would become more menacing, the workload more onerous, petty annoyances more numerous, and the food even worse. Under these circumstances a sailor couldn't resist the temptation of getting away from it all. He deserted—and thereby he lost what wages were due him, and he was subject to arrest, imprisonment, and a forced return to the ship if, for some reason, the captain felt his services were needed for the next lap of the voyage.

Not so in coastal sailing.

Furuseth learned that, because of the unique conditions on the Pacific Coast, sailors did the work of the longshoremen. In the days of the hide and tallow trade, seamen took their vessel close to a ranch where they could load the bundles of hides. In the lumber trade, longshoremen couldn't be waiting at each of the scores of lumber camps at which the vessel put in. The sailors were expected to load the cargo. The Scandinavians on the West Coast didn't mind working hard and fast ("Hurry oop, ve haf to get the loomber on har."), and they appreciated an opportunity to earn wages even after the vessel came into port. They developed skill in handling and stowing lumber.

So, with this knowledge, Furuseth sailed out on a coastal ship. He liked the experience, and never went on a deep water voyage as a seaman again. He received wages of 35 dollars a month instead of 18, wasn't laid off every time his vessel came into port, and was able to enjoy his books and music between voyages.

Most sailors preferred the short coastal voyages, and Furuseth soon learned that because of this he had to be wary of a new danger to sailors that had originated in San Francisco back in early clipper ship times. Trade to the Orient was thriving. When a clipper came around Cape Horn and delivered its cargo in San Francisco, the crimps had trouble rounding up a crew for its next destination: Shanghai. The problem with Shanghai as a destination was that the vessel kept on going westward around the globe. A long time would elapse before it came this way again. So, after the crimps had emptied the boardinghouses, they had to look elsewhere. They went to the waterfront saloons, found their prey, and plied him with liquor or drugs. Or they might sandbag him on the head. The police did little to stop this activity; in fact, they sometimes encouraged it as a means of getting rid of undesirable characters. When the victim woke up he found himself far at sea, with his name forged in the ship's articles, and bound for a long voyage to foreign places. He had been "shanghaied."

For the next four years, Furuseth lived in a San Francisco boardinghouse at 32 Steuart Street, spent much time in the public library, and left occasionally for a short trip on a lumber schooner or to go fishing in Washington or Alaska. He had no problem getting jobs because at that time sailors were in great demand. But, in 1885, economic conditions became depressed, and he couldn't get work. For six weeks, he walked the beach until he finally got employment fishing on the Columbia River. While he was gone, an event took place on the Howard Street Wharf that would change the course of his life.

Chapter Three

During the 1880s, depressed economic conditions, and the visible concentration of wealth and power in the hands of the rich and the corporations, caused a widespread upheaval in the United States. Workers were radicalized, and a wave of unionism swept over the country. In San Francisco, many trades formed unions, including most of the maritime workers. But not the sailors. By the nature of their calling, most were not available for meetings because they were usually away at sea. Despite three attempts, they remained unorganized.

In early 1885, hard times caught up with shipping, sailors' jobs became scarce, and wages were cut to 30 dollars. On March 4th, the shipowners announced that wages would be cut further, from 30 dollars to 25. The seamen refused to accept the cut. They congregated on the waterfront, angry and in a fighting mood. There appeared on the scene Sigismund Danielwicz, a coasting sailor who was a member of the International Workingmen's Association, a radical labor group which was one of the many offshoots of Marx's earlier organization, the First International. An impromptu meeting of the sailors was held one night around the lumber piles on the Howard Street Wharf. Danielwicz urged the men to organize and to strike, promising support from the IWA.

Two days later, on March 6 at 7:30 p.m., a more formal meeting was held on the Folsom Street Wharf to consider a raise of wages to 35 dollars and to take steps to form a permanent union. Burnette Haskell, leader of the IWA in San Francisco, took charge of the meeting. Danielwicz and several other members of the IWA gave speeches, a chairman was elected, and an organizing committee was appointed. Of the 300 sailors attending, 222 enrolled that night, and among them they were able to raise a total of $34.60 for organizing expenses. Haskell donated the use of the IWA offices in Room 69 of the American Building at 6 Eddy Street as the first headquarters of the new union: the Coast Seamen's Union.

A meeting was held in which 456 members accepted a constitution and bylaws submitted by Haskell. Officers were elected, but real control of the union was in the hands of the Advisory Committee which, under the constitution, was to be composed only of members of the IWA.

Furuseth returned from salmon fishing and immediately joined the union ... an act that would set a new course in his life and would affect the lives and well-being of hundreds of thousands of seamen throughout the world.

By July 1, the CSU had 2,000 members, had its own boardinghouse at 217 Broadway, its own hiring hall at 7 Spear Street, and a board-and-batten shack that served as its head-quarters at 513 1/2 East Street. But the crimps and shipowners had no intention of losing control over waterfront hiring. In order to defeat the union, they systematically hired nonunion sailors at lower wages.

Furuseth protested, and argued that these green hands were incapable of handling a sailing ship, as indeed they were. For example, the captain of the barkentine *Quickstick* was furnished with a nonunion crew and tried to get to sea. But he returned in the evening and anchored off Sausalito. "My crew are farmers," he lamented. "They know more about cows than they do about vessels."

When union sailors boarded ships and demanded the removal of scabs, they were met by six-shooters and shotguns. The shipowners exercised their political power by having the city hire a large contingent of extra police to escort the scabs and to harass the union men. The Harbor Police cracked many skulls with nightsticks and pounded many bodies to the ground. For a while, there were regular beatings and sharp scuffles on the waterfront. The union men did their share; scabs were beaten too.

The situation gradually calmed down, and on March 4, 1886, exactly one year after the first meeting by the lumber piles on the Howard Street Wharf, the union had a membership of 3,000. It demanded and got a raise to 35 dollars a month.

But on June 3, an event occurred which proved disastrous for the union:

The Firemen's Union went on strike against the Oceanic Steamship Company, owned by John D. Spreckels. Although the CSU was not directly involved, it chose to join with other unions in a general strike. Not only did the seamen thereby forfeit their wages in accordance with maritime law, but as a consequence of the strike the shipowners banded together to form the powerful Shipowners' Association of the Pacific Coast. The Association issued orders to its captains that thereafter all men were to be hired only through a shipping office established by the Association, and they were to hire only those seamen who had a "grade book" issued by the Association . . . and no grade book would be issued unless the seaman surrendered his union book. This meant that seamen couldn't get jobs unless they renounced their union membership.

Seeing their jobs being taken by deep water sailors, dock

loafers, and farm hands, they decided to strike. The union called out its 3,000 members from all coastwise vessels. There were bloody fights on the waterfront as they tried to prevent scabs from taking jobs through the Association office. Several men were killed. But the Association had the power to starve the union members into submission. Many, desperate for work, quit the union and sailed as nonunion men or took jobs ashore. In desperation, the union officers tried to negotiate with the shipowners, but the owners insisted on complete surrender. Finally, with so many deserters and without funds, the union gave up the fight.

The strike of 1886 had been a disaster for the union. Its membership fell off to about one-third, and its funds were so depleted that the officers even considered having their office telephone disconnected. . . . And wages dropped from 35 dollars a month to as low as 15.

It seemed as though the union was whipped, and in a meeting on August 30, 1886, it was suggested that the union men tear up their cards and ship out at whatever wages they could get. But the minutes of that meeting contains a new name which appeared for the first time. It said simply, "Andrew Furuseth spoke very encouragingly of the present situation." He must also have spoken forcefully because after his speech the union decided to continue the fight.

In January 1887, Rasmus Nielsen, secretary of the union, died. His position was the most important in the union because the office of president had been abolished and the only other paid employees in San Francisco were the patrolmen (business agents). Furuseth was his logical successor. The members looked upon him as a unique sailor. Not only was he literate, but as a member of the Finance Committee he was familiar with the union's financial affairs, and because of his constant reading he had become knowledgeable about history and maritime law. He was elected.

As secretary, he opened the mail, collected dues, kept the financial records, took care of all correspondence, examined applicants for membership, paid bills, acted as liaison with other unions, and took care of members' grievances and anything else that needed doing. In short, other than the duties performed by the patrolmen, Furuseth ran the union . . . but all under the control of the Advisory Committee. He had no family and no special interests except reading to distract him, so he devoted 14 to 16 hours a day to his job. In return, he received wages of 13 dollars a week.

Determined to expand the union and to restore morale, he started a dynamic program. The union began to publish its own newspaper, the Coast Seamen's Journal, in order to plead its cause before the public and to keep its own membership informed.

Seamen were still being arrested as criminals for "deserting" a vessel before the end of a voyage; they were still being held aboard as slaves. In Furuseth's reading of maritime law and court cases, he discovered a means of correcting this injustice. The courts held a seaman guilty because he had breached the terms of the Articles of Agreement, a contract between himself and the vessel, which under the provisions of the Shipping Commissioners' Act of 1872 made him subject to criminal penalties for desertion.

This Act of 1872 was repealed by the Act of 1874. In order to save time and money, the shipowners had objected to the inconvenience of signing men on and off before a commissioner on the short coastal runs. They persuaded Congress to eliminate the requirement for signing Articles on these short trips.

In his extensive reading, Furuseth discovered that when the courts began to interpret the Act of 1874, they read it literally. And he reasoned that if the coasting crew didn't have to sign Articles, there were no Articles for them to breach! Furuseth realized that the unintended result was to make the coasting sailor a free man. He could now quit his vessel, just as any worker on land could quit his job, without fear of being arrested, detained, and surrendered back to the ship.

Furuseth reported this to the membership, and suggested that they engage in an action that became known as the "Oracle," and which worked like this: In order to be hired, the union men accepted the "grade books" issued by the Association in exchange for their union books, and went aboard a vessel. But just before it was to sail, they tossed their belongings onto the dock and left the ship. The sailors now had the "right" to quit, so the captain could do nothing but delay the sailing until he could hire another crew. Often the new crew would repeat the action and the ship would be held up for a few more days, each delay resulting in further financial losses for the shipowners. When the losses became more than they could bear, the shipowners knew they had been outfoxed, and gave up the fight. No longer did they require an Association "grade book" as a condition of employment. Once again, they hired union men . . . and at increased wages—Furuseth's first major victory for the seamen.

Furuseth was to have many victories, and many defeats, but this victory must have been especially satisfying. For ages, "poor Jack" had been stepped upon, had been taken advantage of, with no chance to protect himself. But now, because of Furuseth's reading, because of his analysis of the 1874 Act and of his thinking, he had devised a means to fight back. The "Oracle" had defeated the "grade book." At last, the sailors had won a battle.

But in his efforts to enhance and protect the rights of sailors, it wasn't just the shipowners that Furuseth had to fight. There were others.

He objected to the influence that Burnette Haskell and the other socialist members of the International Workingmen's Association had over the union. Although they were devoted and active members of the union, he felt they often led it astray with their socialist ideas. Furuseth was an uncompromising individualist. In his travels he had developed an overwhelming and perhaps prejudicial aversion to socialists. Right or wrong, he was stubborn in his refusal to see any merit in their goals. He was convinced they were up to no good. And the IWW was full of "radicals" who controlled the union through the Advisory Committee. They must be stopped.

So, Furuseth objected to the rule that only members of the IWA could be on the Advisory Committee. He knew it would be difficult to get rid of them because most had given up sailing and were now employed on shore. They could come to every meeting, while most of the "real" sailors seldom attended because they were out at sea. Furuseth tried to get rid of Haskell with gentle prodding and political maneuvering, without success. But ultimately, he and other conservative leaders persuaded the union members to change the bylaws to provide that the Advisory Committee was open to any member of the union, and then to abolish the Committee entirely. Furuseth took full control of the union, breaking the hold of the IWA.

This was only the first of many battles Furuseth was to have with "radicals." This time he had won, but there were more to come. Eventually, they would crush him.

Another problem arose. Shipowners were gradually converting from sailing ships to steam vessels. The Coast Seamen's Union, which was composed entirely of men who manned sailing ships, regarded steamship sailors with contempt. To them, the steamer was "not a ship, but a floating blacksmith's shop." The men who went to sea in such craft knew nothing about sails; they were just "seagoing mechanics." So the union made no effort to organize them. However, Burnette Haskell formed a union for the steamship seamen. Conflict between the two unions began almost immediately. On the few occasions when a vessel was converted from sail to steam, the two unions fought. These jurisdictional fights continued until July 29, 1891, when Furuseth negotiated an agreement which joined the two unions into one. Since that time it has been called the Sailors' Union of the Pacific.

Jurisdictional problems were no novelty to Furuseth. From the moment he became a coastal sailor, he fought the longshoremen over who would load and discharge cargo. Furuseth and most sailors felt a deep-seated distrust of all people on shore. The sailor was constantly taken advantage of by unscrupulous crimps, boardinghouse keepers, prostitutes, and other land people, and he learned to distrust them all.

With all these distractions, Furuseth still managed to get members to return to the union, to rebuild the treasury, and to restore morale. Wages had risen, the grade book system had been abolished, and the sailors' union was the only union with a newspaper of its own. After two years as secretary, Furuseth yearned to return to the sea. Also, he believed in limited tenure for officials, so he told the members he would not run for election again. He left the union with the records in perfect order, a membership of over 2,000, and a treasury of 22,000 dollars.

For almost two years, he sailed and fished, contented as long as he had tobacco for his pipe and a book to read. But in early 1891, the union had problems. The treasurer (a new union officer) had "borrowed" union funds, and the secretary, Henry Ark, disappeared, along with 2,000 dollars of union money. After Ark was caught and sentenced to San Quentin, the Coast Seamen's Journal reported that "The story is briefly told, an unscrupulous woman and an infatuated weak man."

Some members pleaded with Furuseth to return and run for secretary again. Reluctantly, he did, and won the office by a vote of 219 to 62. Less than a year later, he submitted his resignation and shipped out on a fishing boat. But, within two months the union asked him to come back. Once again, he answered the call. But this time the man who favored limited tenure held the office for an additional 44 years, until 1936.

He was now 38 years old, and he had a rather plump face and a prominent nose. His brown hair, with a part on the right side, had a slight wave. His mouth drooped slightly at the corners. Someone who knew him at that time described him as "long-limbed, loose-jointed, carrying himself with a sailor's purposefulness rather than with a landsman's pride. . . . His face (gives the) impression of a courageous but conciliatory disposition. There is doubtless emotion enough in him, somewhere, but his surface appearance is one of pure thought . . . What at first puzzles you is the absence from his talk of anything like the emotional exaggeration of the labor leader."

In several respects he was unlike the other labor leaders.

Union work was hard and required a rare mental quality, so labor leaders received generous salaries. But Furuseth refused to accept any salary higher than the earnings of an able-bodied seaman.

"The only man who can do anything for his fellow man," Furuseth said, "is the man who has nothing and wants nothing for himself."

The highest salary he ever accepted in his entire career was 75 dollars a month.

"So live that you may have nothing to lose" was a principle of his life.

Furuseth sought to improve the reputation of the union and to develop a better relationship with the shipowners. He argued that if the union wanted to do business with employers, it had to operate on business principles and with a sense of fairness. He felt a sailor who reported for work drunk, or failed to show up for work, or lacked adequate skill, was a reflection on the union. He stressed the high moral principles of the trade union movement. He tried to be even-handed, occasionally going along with the employers when he thought they were in the right.

We have evidence of this from the words of Peter B. Kyne, the author, who once worked on the San Francisco waterfront, but on the side of the shipowners. He had heard of Furuseth "and nothing good of him, either. He was a Radical, a disturber of the maritime status quo, an insolent fellow who dared to tell the bosses how many hours their employees should work and for how much." The two men met on unfriendly terms.

But Kyne grew to admire Furuseth, and remained his friend right up to the end. In later years he wrote that Andrew Furuseth "was the most honest and fearless man I ever knew. He kept his covenants and expected his sailors to do the same."

Kyne related how occasionally a few sailors would try to claim overtime that was not due them. Just before the vessel was set to sail, they would quit work and just stand on the dock, hoping the captain, to save the loss from demurrage, would call them back and approve their unjust claims. Kyne wrote, "I used to bring the payroll down to the vessel and hang around. Whenever one of these outlaw strikes was pulled I would telephone Andy . . . I can see him now walking up the Embarcadero with long strides, his ill-fitting suit flapping around him, his brown derby down on his ears, in his eyes the flame of the zealot, looking neither to left nor right . . . The sight of that gaunt figure hurrying to the fray would send the strikers back on the job and the ship would be moving away before Andy could come aboard. But from the dock he'd shake his fist at the men who had let him down, promising to discipline them when they returned to port."

Unfortunately, the sailors didn't always respond to these noble sentiments, and the employers didn't hesitate to take advantage of any opportunity that came their way.

Just before the general business depression of 1893, the shipping business declined, and there was a surplus of seamen. So, the Association reopened its own shipping office and hired only men who would sail for less than union rates. And it also reinstituted the "grade book", which union sailors hated because the book not only listed the sailor's sea service record, but it was also used to blacklist him.

The sailors responded by reinstituting the "Oracle." That is, they hired on a vessel, and then jumped ship just before she was set to sail, causing a delay and a financial loss to the shipowners. At the first sign of trouble, Furuseth warned the members to exercise caution so that the responsibility for any conflict would not rest on the union. When the "Oracle" failed, the union men ignored Furuseth's warning. They boarded ships and beat up the scabs.

The employers retaliated by hiring G.C. Williams as secretary of the Shipowners' Association. It was later learned that the name Williams was an alias, that he was wanted by the Michigan police on a charge of bribery, and that he was guilty of perjury on other occasions. He expressed his method of breaking the union by the statement, "A dose of cold lead has a wonderful effect in quieting disorders."

As a result, the year 1892 saw East Street the scene of more bloodshed than ever. Crimps and shipowners were as ruthless as the union seamen. Crimps and their runners lurked along the fringes of the Barbary Coast, lying in wait for union men. Each morning dawned on beaten, sometimes lifeless, bodies.

The Harbor Police were powerless to check the series of riots, beatings, sabotage, and murders that swept the waterfront.

The cables of the nonunion full-rigged ship *Tacoma* were sawed and the vessel allowed to drift out to sea. Dynamite was found on the British tramp steamer *Bawnmore* and the tugs *Ethel* and *Marian*. The union denied all knowledge of such incidents, and claimed the crimps and the shipowners had probably carried out these provocations in order to blame them on the union. The union appealed for public support.

The 1893 depression hit hard across the country. The union lost its battle. Wages were lowered, the union treasury was drained, and its membership declined.

Still more trouble came. After an evening of carousing, six nonunion scab sailors were returning to the boardinghouse of Johnny Curtin, a well-known crimp. The time was after midnight. One of the sailors, Curtin's son, saw a small black valise in the entrance way. He picked it up, quickly dropped it, and ran away, shouting, "It's dynamite." A tremendous explosion shook the neighborhood, blowing out the front of the building and instantly killing five.

Furuseth was immediately questioned by the police, who assumed, as did the newspapers and the public, that the union was responsible. Furuseth called it "the most dastardly crime ever committed on the waterfront," and argued that the union had nothing to gain from such a vile deed. But even when subsequent arrests and trials failed to show any connection between the union and the bombing, there was no use in claiming innocence—how could he prove a negative? Whatever public sympathy that had existed for "poor Jack" in his fight against the unpopular Employers' Association disappeared when the bomb exploded.

With Furuseth's union collapsing and the public turned against it, a lesser man might have succumbed to a period of depression, but with a stubborn determination Furuseth wrote a message of courage and hope to the membership. "(L)ike a clap of thunder from the clear sky came the dynamite outrage setting the whole city against us. We are innocent ... but it is there and must be reckoned with in all our dealings for the future . . . (S)ince we do submit we do so without grumbling or crying . . . that is our lot at present . . . Let us comrades take our medicine like stoics and from our trouble shall we rise again."

Setback after setback did not crush him. Often he would say, "*Tomorrow is also a day**. We will start all over again. We will work harder."

---

* A few years after Furuseth's death, a letter was written by Mae E. Waggaman, who worked for him as his secretary in Washington. She wrote, "For many years I have been connected with the labor movement and have worked with lawyers and newspapermen, but have never worked for a man who had such determination to win; more enduring patience; nor a more humble and self-sacrificing nature than Andrew Furuseth. He had many disappointments but he never seemed to be discouraged; he would always say, 'Tomorrow is also a Day.'"

Chapter Four

Meanwhile, Furuseth was struggling with another problem. Previously, the union had been almost powerless in using the strike tactic as a means of improving wages and working conditions. At no time could it have the entire membership behind it, because about 60 per cent of the men were at sea under contract, and about 15 to 20 per cent were on board vessels in harbors under contract. If they tried to join in the strike, they could be imprisoned for desertion. This meant that there were only 20 to 25 per cent of the unemployed members on shore to fight for better conditions.

But the situation had changed when Furuseth discovered the flaw in the 1874 Act. When the shipowners encouraged Congress to dispense with the requirement that seamen sign articles on the short coastal voyages, Furuseth had seized the opportunity. With no articles to sign, there were no articles to breach, so the sailor was free to leave the ship if he chose to. This flaw, together with the use of the Oracle, had given the union some power to fight back. There was hope for better days.

It didn't take the shipowners long to correct this error on their part. They went to Congress and secured passage of a law requiring all coasting seamen to sign articles, and thus to again be subject to the criminal penalties of the 1872 Act.

Furuseth's euphoric satisfaction in having made a gain, collapsed into gloom. His first major victory for the seamen had been snatched away. They were no closer to freedom than they had ever been.

Furuseth lamented, "We hold up our manacled hands."

One of the other officers of the union suggested that their efforts should be concentrated on pushing for higher wages and other typical union goals. Furuseth answered, "No, let's get the seamen *free* first. Then they can do what they damn well please."

But how could the seamen get free? Whenever they took a step forward, the shipowners got Congress to change the laws, and so pushed them back again.

. . . the laws . . . the laws

Like a burst of sunlight, the answer flashed in Furuseth's mind. Two could play at the game. Why not get the laws changed to suit the sailors instead of the shipowners?

Legislation!

As a first step, he had the Sailors' Union of the Pacific elect a legislative committee that under Furuseth's direction prepared "An Appeal to Congress." It recommended amendments to the Shipping Commissioners' Act to include eliminating involuntary servitude, requiring the vessels to carry a full crew at all times, improving small and badly ventilated forecastles, making the vessel liable for any cruelties inflicted upon the men by the officers, and providing the means to correct almost 30 other grievances.

Furuseth had to look for help. Seamen's unions had been formed on the Atlantic Coast, the Gulf, and the Great Lakes. He met Samuel Gompers, leader of the American Federation of Labor. Furuseth outlined his plans for a national organization of seamen, and on April 22, 1892, the National Seamen's Union of America was formally organized, and later became affiliated with the AFL. (Shortly thereafter, it changed its name to the International Seamen's Union of America.) In

1895, the ISU elected Furuseth to be in Washington to look after legislation of interest to the seamen. But due to business and shipping stagnation, and owing to the lack of funds on the part of affiliated unions, the ISU didn't get beyond the paper stage for several years. In 1899, it had very few members and no activity.

Meanwhile, back in California, Furuseth found the help he needed. He spoke to James G. Maguire, Democratic candidate for Congress from the Fourth District. The union had a policy of staying out of politics, but Furuseth got the union to endorse Maguire. He stubbornly denied that the endorsement was an exception to the "no politics" rule; it was merely "support of the union's legislative program," which Maguire had endorsed.

The action proved to be a wise and fortunate one. Maguire—a former Assemblyman, Superior Court judge, and a practicing lawyer—was elected, and he pushed the seamen's program faithfully and energetically. He divided the program into six bills, and introduced them in Congress. He asked that the SUP send a representative to Washington to explain the bills. W.J.B.Mackay, a competent native American seaman, was considered the best choice because he was the type most likely to influence congressmen. But at the last moment he couldn't go, so half by accident Furuseth was sent instead. Furuseth, the man who wore a rumpled suit which he washed instead of sending to the cleaners (and which he pressed sailor-style: that is, laid out between the mattress and bed boards overnight). He, who spoke with the wavering lilt of a Norwegian immigrant, and who spoke of "yustice" and "yail." Did he have the qualifications of a lobbyist? Was he competent to speak before a congressional committee in the nation's capitol?

When Furuseth came to Washington, he was shadowed

by detectives, who followed his every move. The Pacific Coast shipowners had warned the Washington police that he was a dangerous anarchist. Several years passed before Furuseth was allowed to move about the nation's capitol free from police surveillance.

He tried to visit other congressmen to gain support. But as soon as the receptionist saw the tall man with the lean, zealous face and the cheap unpressed suit, she remembered that the congressman was out of town.

Furuseth testified before the House Committee on Merchant Marine and Fisheries. He was shocked at the ignorance of congressmen on maritime matters. The shipowners flooded Congress with mail, denouncing the Maguire bills as "arbitrary and unjust," as well as "communistic and subversive." The first bill was killed in committee by a filibuster, but Furuseth was not discouraged. He saw that the congressmen had been impressed with the seamen's cause and seemed ready to learn more.

There was a further hearing, and Maguire asked the SUP to send a union representative to give the bill support. Neither the SUP nor the National Seamen's Union could afford the expense, but Samuel Gompers used AFL funds to buy Furuseth's railroad ticket to Washington and to pay his expenses while there. The bill passed Congress and was signed by President Cleveland on February 18, 1895. It abolished imprisonment for "desertion" from coastwise vessels, exempted a seaman's clothing from attachment, and prohibited the advance on the payment of wages. A big step forward.

But other abuses still needed correction. Deep water sailors could still be guilty of "desertion," shanghaiing remained a common custom, food was still often inedible, scurvy and beriberi were rampant, sailors were still beaten,

forecastles were still small and unhealthy, and other grievances still needed to be rectified.

Furuseth again took the long train ride to Washington in
late 1895 to get prepared for the congressional hearings on the
remaining Maguire bills. Although he was provided with a
comparatively liberal expense account, he scrimped as tightly
as he could, walked miles to save taxi fares, and brought the
savings back to the union treasury. He rented a cubbyhole of
a bedroom at the third-rate Keystone Hotel. Up at 5 a.m. each
morning, he went to a restaurant for his favorite breakfast of
coffee and Danish pastry, and then spent his day writing
letters, talking to congressmen, reading maritime law, and
attending hearings. He spent lonely evenings in his bare hotel
room preparing for the next day's work. Persons living in the
neighborhood sometimes complained to the hotel about
someone who disturbed their sleep by pounding on a type-
writer until 3 o'clock or 4 in the morning. The sailor had
learned to type.

Meanwhile, back in San Francisco, another man was
also writing. Furuseth had chosen a young Scotch sailor,
Walter Macarthur, as editor of the *Coast Seamen's Journal*.
Sitting in the Union's little office on East Street, Macarthur
read through back numbers of the *Journal*, filled with reports
of brutality at sea. The public didn't know, or didn't believe,
such things possible. So Macarthur began publishing a supple-
ment, a chronicle of some of the most notable cases of abuse
suffered by the sailors between 1888 and 1895. After running
in several installments, and with the financial help of the
National Seamen's Union, the articles were bound and published in the form of a pamphlet entitled *The Red Record*. Its
striking cover, printed in bright red ink, depicted a hand
gripping a blood-covered belaying pin. It described 64 cases of

violence by bucko mates and calloused captains against the sailors. It included such incidents as being tied to a stanchion four days and kept without food; being knocked down, jumped upon, and dying the next day; loss of eyes, limbs, and teeth; a sick man hauled out of his bunk and made to go aloft (as Furuseth had been forced to do in his early sailing days); being triced up, with toes barely touching the deck; broken noses and dislocated shoulders; and similar cruelties.

The roster included 14 deaths "under circumstances which justify the charge of murder," but only three convictions for brutality were secured, with minor punishment. The rest were either dismissed on the ground of "lack of evidence," or, if tried, they were exonerated because of "justifiable discipline."

Furuseth didn't believe that this cruelty was motivated solely by malice, but was rather a symptom of a much more serious malady. In many cases the buckoes, with the ship's safety in mind, acted this way to discipline inexperienced men and loafers who were hired through the crimping system. Furuseth believed that most of the problems could be solved if Congress would make the sailor a free man. If the sailor were free, the power of the crimps would be destroyed, only qualified seamen would sail the ships, and there would be no need for cruel punishment.

Furuseth arranged to have *The Red Record* sent to periodicals, to every congressman, and to other public figures. It was reprinted in various publications. Its revelations caught the public's attention and proved to be a powerful weapon.

The shipowners had weapons of their own. They conceded to themselves that Furuseth was the most intelligent sailor they had ever met, so they assembled their strongest forces to oppose him at the congressional hearings on the remaining Maguire bills.

Following are a few excerpts from the transcripts of the hearings, to show the shipowners' attitude toward seamen, and Furuseth's ability to stand up to them.

Vernon C. Brown, president of the Maritime Exchange of New York, was their principal spokesman. At one of the hearings he testified, " . . . I will state a proposition which I think nobody will deny or seek to refute: That these seamen on board vessels of the United States are the wards of the nation; that they are men incapable of making civil contracts of a kind American citizens are capable of making. They are taken care of the same as orphans are. Special legislation stands on the statute books today to safeguard their interests and to take care of them." So that his opinion would be clearly understood, he added, "They are driftwood from their native countries where they cannot get employment, and drift here . . . Their average intelligence is very low . . . "

One of the committeemen said, "Mr. Furuseth is a seaman. Does he not show evidence of intelligence?"

Brown replied, "That is a matter of opinion."

When the subject of the hearing turned to whether sailors should be imprisoned for desertion, Brown testified that " . . . we are willing to accept, in lieu of imprisonment . . . a provision granting the master . . . the authority and power to apprehend such deserting seaman . . . and take him back on board the vessel."

To which Furuseth replied, "If we must have one of the two, we had rather take the humanity of the jail."

During one part of the hearings, Furuseth was arguing that the crimps could be rid of only if the allotment or advance payment system was eliminated. The chairman posed a question to Furuseth. Suppose there was no allotment. A man could lose his money in a few minutes. Suppose the sailor gambled his money away, was destitute for money, and couldn't get an advance. What then?

Furuseth answered, "The best thing that can be done with him and the kindest action you can take with him is to say, 'My boy, starve until you learn how to behave yourself.'"

Another issue was the amount of space to be allotted to each seaman in the forecastle. Furuseth proposed 120 cubic feet; the Commissioner of Navigation proposed 72, which Furuseth claimed was "a little too large for a coffin, but surely not large enough for a living man."

During the hearings, despite his Norwegian accent and his ungraceful appearance, Furuseth spoke and acted as a full-fledged lawyer. He knew the rules of evidence. ("The burden of proof, I believe, Mr. Chairman, is always on those who bring the suit. Surely it is not on the defendant.") He cited court cases, and seemed to know the facts and holdings of each case he cited. He referred to sections of the statutes and, without copies before him, was able to describe the contents of the sections, often quoting parts verbatim.

Furuseth remained in Washington for seven months, planning, pleading, and explaining. Two more of the Maguire bills were reported out and sent to the Senate for approval.

When Furuseth returned to San Francisco in June 1896, he found the SUP rapidly disintegrating. Frequently, a quorum couldn't be gathered, meetings were short, and funds were low. The shipowners had signed a formal agreement with the boardinghouse keepers to freeze the union off the waterfront; the owners agreed to hire only through the boardinghouses, who in return promised to refuse rooms to any men who went on strike.

Already, some union members were complaining that Furuseth spent too much time in Washington and not enough in San Francisco. But Furuseth felt strongly that the local problems were only symptoms; they were the consequences of fundamental problems, and that those problems could be solved only through congressional legislation. He felt that is where he should concentrate his efforts. After all, hadn't the first Maguire bill been signed into law? And when the others were adopted by Congress, the local problems would resolve themselves.

It was at this time that Furuseth was stunned by one of the biggest disappointments of his life.

After the passage of the first Maguire bill, seamen generally believed that they could leave vessels in ports on the Pacific Coast when dissatisfied with their employment, without fear of imprisonment. But the powerful shipping interests were not prepared to give up without a struggle. They found an opportunity, and exploited it.

Four seamen signed articles before a shipping commissioner in San Francisco to sail on the barkentine *Arago* to Knappton, Washington, at the mouth of the Columbia River, where she would load lumber; then to Valparaiso, Chile; finally to return to San Francisco. When the ship arrived in Knappton, the sailors had been dissatisfied with conditions on board ship and didn't want to continue on the foreign voyage. So they left the vessel in Knappton. They were arrested and locked up in jail for 16 days. When the *Arago* was ready to put to sea, they were brought on board against their will by a United States marshall. At sea, they refused to obey the command of the master to turn to, so they were put in chains. On arrival in San Francisco, they were imprisoned in the Alameda County jail.

At their trial, the lower court held that although arrested in a domestic coast port, the seamen had signed articles for a foreign voyage, and therefore they were not protected by the Maguire Act. The significance of this was that if a seaman could be arrested when the articles included a non-American port, it would be a simple matter to insert such a port in all articles of agreement, including coast runs, and the Maguire Act would be worthless

Pending the trial, a writ of habeas corpus was applied for on the ground that the seamen were placed aboard the *Arago* against their will and therefore contrary to the 13th Amendment of the Federal Constitution, which prohibits involuntary servitude.

The writ was denied.

An appeal was taken, and the U.S. Supreme Court sustained the lower court. The Supreme Court referred to the maritime law of the ancient Rhodians, which antedated the birth of Christ by about 900 years, and other long-standing laws. It held that the seaman's contract, based upon ancient maritime laws, was different from other contracts . . . and that the 13th Amendment was intended to apply only to Negro slaves, and *not* to seamen! The sailor's "surrender of personal liberty" remained unchanged.

And this in a country in which "all men are created equal."

This time Furuseth came closer to being completely crushed than at any other time in his life. He couldn't believe what the Court had ruled. His sailors had less rights than the Negroes. Less rights than anybody. In fact, they had *no* rights.

Furuseth felt the shocking setback deeply. An event occurred a few months later which might serve as a clue to the impact on his feelings. The Grand Marshall of the Fourth of July parade in San Francisco invited the Sailors' Union to participate. Perhaps the sarcastic tone of Furuseth's reply is evidence of the lingering bitterness he must have felt.

"(B)eing mindful of our status . . . that of involuntary servitude . . . felt it would be an imposition on our part to . . . inflict our presence . . . the presence of bondsmen . . . upon the freemen who will on the Fourth of July celebrate their freedom."

A year later, after the Supreme Court refused a new hearing, Furuseth again declined an invitation to celebrate Independence Day. He declared that "the spectacle of a slave worshipping his chains would be less ludicrous than that of the American seaman celebrating Independence Day."

The scene around the old San Francisco Ferry House, as it appeared to Furuseth when he arrived in 1880.

Unloading lumber from a coastal ship.

An apple peddler on East Street at the Howard Street Wharf.

Sailors milling about in front of the Sailors' Union headquarters on Steuart Street.

Nephew 493 Penna Ave. Washington, D.C.

This is believed to be a rare photo, apparently taken when Furuseth first went to Washington, D.C. It was discovered recently among papers he had left with a friend.

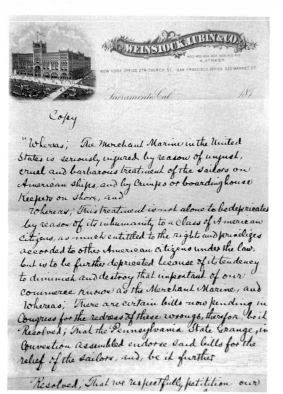

Weinstock, Lubin & Co.
400 402 404 406 408 410 412 K. STREET
NEW YORK OFFICE 274 CHURCH ST.   SAN FRANCISCO OFFICE 523 MARKET ST.

Sacramento, Cal. ___ 189_

Copy

"Whereas; The Merchant Marine in the United
States is seriously injured by reason of unjust,
cruel and barbarous treatment of the sailors on
American ships, and by Crimps or boardinghouse
Keepers on shore, and

Whereas; This treatment is not alone to be deprecated
by reason of its inhumanity to a class of American
citizens, as much entitled to the rights and privileges
accorded to other American citizens under the law,
but is to be further deprecated because of its tendency
to diminish and destroy that important of our
commerce known as the Merchant Marine, and

Whereas; There are certain bills now pending in
Congress for the redress of these wrongs, therefore be it
Resolved; That the Pennsylvania State Grange, in
Convention assembled endorse said bills for the
relief of the sailors, and, be it further

Resolved; That we respectfully petition our

Furuseth wrote hundreds
of petitions, letters,
articles, etc. to further the
sailors' cause.

He instilled pride in the men. They marched proudly in their blue and white dress
uniforms.

Senator Robert M. LaFollette
who, together with Furuseth,
freed the sailors through the
enactment of the Seamen's
Act of 1915.

Only after the passage of the
Seamen's Act would Furuseth
consent to have his public photo
taken.

The old Viking hung on, despite his age and illness.

Harry Lundeberg, who would take over the wheel as head of the Sailors' Union of the Pacific.

The 1934 Maritime Strike began with a picket line on the Embarcadero.

Photos on this page: The Bancroft Library, University of California, Berkeley

Furuseth (at the extreme right, holding a cigar) enjoyed his last victory: the burning of the fink hall books.

Chapter Five

As a result of his intensive reading, Furuseth mastered the English language and in due course attained an eloquence in formal oratory. His clear, meaningful, and effective speech held his audience. His strong Norwegian accent in which every "j" sounded like a "y" never seemed to bother him or make him self-conscious. He was completely at ease at the platform.

On the one-to-one level, Furuseth could speak in the language of the coarsest sailor. But he was also able to converse on equal terms with shipowners, congressmen, and senators. He eventually proved he could hold his own when speaking to the President of the United States.

He spent much of his time writing. His letters tended to be lengthy—eight, 10, 15 single-spaced typewritten pages—but they were nevertheless concise and logical. In those days letter writing was an art, and people took the time to read and to digest what they read. Furuseth also wrote dozens of pamphlets, addresses, and essays, all of which exhibited a rare clearness, vividness, and power.

His reading included maritime law, history, philosophy, Norwegian classics, and Shakespeare. He was an avid and lifelong student of the Bible. Out of this he hammered out a philosophy of his own. It centered around sailors' desire to be free, coupled with their training that they must work together to keep their vessel shipshape and afloat. They must be organized. He believed strongly in the trade union movement. But he didn't like the type of organization Haskell and the other socialists advocated, with their utopian schemes and their attempts to form a labor party. Furuseth believed the solution lay in developing a strong union that could influence the already established political parties to support the sailors' cause.

He usually spent the evenings in his room on Steuart Street, reading, writing, thinking. Occasionally, he returned to his room too tired to read or write. Then he took out from his suitcase a needle and black thread. Like most sailors, without a wife or any other woman to help him, Furuseth was handy with the needle. Sometimes he mended his clothes, but sometimes he took out a piece of white linen cloth, about 16 inches by 18, and slowly, deliberately began to ... embroider with cross-stitches! Not designs, but words ... A message in words ... Norwegian words. At this time he already had part of it done: *"Saa har Gud elsket ... "*

Although Furuseth always considered himself first and foremost a member of the SUP, it was inevitable that his unique abilities and interests would cause him to use his energy not only on local matters, but also on issues of national and international concern. His vehicle was the International Seamen's Union which he had helped form in 1892. Although the ISU was fairly weak in its first years, from 1900 to 1903 its membership grew to almost 20,000. Furuseth was elected president from 1892 until his death well into the next century, except for a few intervening years.

However, Furuseth realized he couldn't, through seamen's unions alone, accomplish the goals he had set. Seamen had no political power because most of them didn't stay ashore long enough in one place to meet the residency requirements under the states' voting laws. And even if they did qualify as voters, they were often at sea when the voting took place. So Furuseth affiliated the ISU with the American Federation of Labor. And it was in his role as ISU representative that he participated in the affairs of the AFL, to which he devoted much of his time and through which he became a national figure.

Samuel Gompers, president of the AFL, had a philosophy of unionism as conservative as Furuseth's. He distrusted intellectual reformers, radicalism, and irresponsible strikes. He strove to make unionism respectable, and he admired Furuseth. At a sailors' meeting he praised their leader: "Furuseth has stood at the doors of the Capitol, like a panther watching, like a lion attacking. No scheme has been hatched against you that he has not exposed, and by exposing it, defeated it."

Furuseth became active in the AFL. He attended every annual convention from 1893 to 1936, with two exceptions. He was regularly elected either chairman or secretary of the Committee on the President's Report, one of the most important convention committees. He introduced resolutions pertaining to seamen's legislation, but also resolutions of more general labor interest, such as international affairs, arbitration, and injunctions. He was particularly active in attempting to abolish the use of injunctions in labor disputes. True to character, he studied the subject in such depth that few people, either in Congress or the labor movement, knew as much about injunctions as he. Furuseth gave much to the AFL, and, on the other hand, Gompers swung the whole force and influence of the AFL behind legislation Furuseth sought for the benefit of his sailors.

And plenty of help was needed.

The *Arago* case that held the constitutional provision against involuntary servitude did not apply to seamen, shocked

Furuseth, but it only made him more determined to change the law. Senator Stephen White of California introduced a bill embodying the seamen's major demands. Furuseth plunged into activities in support of the bill, writing letters, holding mass meetings, visiting congressmen and senators. After delays and amendments, and with the help of the AFL, the White Bill became law in December 1898. It did provide for the right to quit work in any American port, and a few other improvements, but it still allowed imprisonment for an American seaman's desertion in a foreign port and for a foreign seaman's desertion in an American port. There was still much work to be done.

Although San Francisco was Furuseth's official residence, he travelled by train to Washington every December and remained for a few months. His abode there was a simple, bare room in the attic of the old National Hotel on Pennsylvania Avenue.

Except when attending AFL conventions or other conferences, every day he would be at the ISU office early to read mail and to dictate letters. Often he would bring to the office a six or eight page article, written in his room the night before, to be typed in proper form by his secretary. He attended congressional hearings, conferred with other labor leaders, visited congressmen. His days were full.

But he spent most of the long winter evenings in his hotel room . . . alone.

Furuseth began to spend more and more of his time in Washington, but he remained in constant communication with the Sailors' Union of the Pacific. He received the minutes of every meeting, and he retained the office of secretary, although most of the work was done by an assistant in his absence.

Upon his return from the East, Furuseth usually made a visit to all locals, from Seattle to San Pedro. He reported on the progress of his legislative efforts and discussed local problems. At his San Francisco office, he drove himself as hard as he did in Washington. With a cigar or pipe hanging from his mouth, he kept busy typing his own letters to congressmen, government officials, and union officers. Occasionally, he would pass an evening at the home of one of the other union officers, but, as in Washington, most evenings he was alone.

He had become well-known by thousands of sailors along the West Coast, including a young sailor named Jack London. Whether the two men ever met, we don't know. But it seems quite possible that London not only knew about Furuseth, but that he based some of his writings on him.

In London's *The Sea Wolf*, Wolf Larsen, one of the most unforgettable characters in literature, is an enigma. On the one hand, he is a savage, Nietzschean superman, the epitome of the most brutal of the buckoes. On the other hand, he is a well-read, articulate philosopher. Van Weyden, the protagonist in the novel, experiences the dark side of Wolf Larsen. Then one day he enters Larsen's stateroom and is surprised to see books of Shakespeare, Tennyson, Poe, and Spencer. Later, he and Wolf Larsen engage in long discussions, philosophizing on immortality, altrusim, hedonism. "We fell into discussions," he says. "Philosophy, science, evolution, religion." Van Weyden remarks of Larsen, "How clearly he thought, and how well he expressed what he thought." It seems likely that London based this side of Wolf Larsen on what he had learned about Furuseth.

Wolf Larsen was said to have been born in Norway, near Romsdal Fjord. (Furuseth was born in Romedal.)

In the very first sentence of *The Sea Wolf*, in which

London had to think up a name for a minor character, he wrote, "I scarcely know where to begin, though I sometimes facetiously place the cause of it all to Charley Furuseth's credit." (Furuseth is certainly not a common name.)

How accurately London describes Furuseth when he says of Wolf Larsen, "He is certainly an individualist of the most pronounced type. Not only that, but he is very lonely. There is no congeniality between him and the rest of the men aboard ship. His tremendous virity and mental strength wall him apart."

Then London strikes at the very heart of Furuseth's being, with a description characteristic of a common Norwegian trait: "This loneliness is bad enough in itself, but to make it worse, he is oppressed by the primal melancholy of the race. Knowing him, I review the old Scandinavian myths with clearer understanding . . . And it is a sadness as deep-reaching as the roots of the race. It is the race heritage, the sadness which has made the race sober-minded, clean-lived, and fanatically moral."

London concludes his observation with, "In point of fact, the chief vent to this primal melancholy has been religion in its most agonizing forms. But the compensations of such religion are denied Wolf Larsen. His brutal materialism will not permit it."

However, the description fits Furuseth to a T, and it would explain why he so obsessively devoted his life to a single cause. It seems evident that London knew Furuseth, and that he understood him.

By 1900, San Francisco had changed its appearance, if not its character, from what it was when Furuseth arrived 20 years before. The old wooden Ferry House had been razed, and in its place stood the grand new Ferry Building, with a handsome 235-foot tower modeled after the Giralda Tower in Seville, Spain. Horse-drawn streetcars still made the turn in front of the Ferry Building, but now they were joined by trolley cars that were powered by electricity. A new type of building had appeared: steel-frame structures that towered above their neighbors and added a striking new note to the downtown skyline.

North of Market Street, the more prosperous citizens built their homes on Nob and Russian Hills, along Van Ness Avenue, and in the Pacific Heights area. South of Market, rows of modest wooden houses of the working class spread over and around the intervening hills, creeping westward toward the ocean, and swinging to the south. Building associations bought large tracts of land in outlying districts, subdivided them into 25-foot lots, and built hundreds of houses of uniform design: two-story residences with gabled roofs and bay windows (called "flats" by the locals), and adorned by a profusion of millwork ("gingerbread").

The waterfront had also changed. Gone were the lumber yards and hay barns on the blocks between Steuart and East Streets, from Market to Howard. The land was now occupied by some maritime mercantile buildings, but mostly sailors' boarding houses and cheap hotels, with saloons on every corner and a few in between. The most striking change took place on the south side of Mission, between Steuart and East Streets. Hippolite d'Audiffred, a Frenchman, bought the land, had the dilapidated shacks torn down, and built the Audiffred Building, a three-story brick structure with a distinctive mansard roof. The ground floor of the Mission-East Streets corner was occupied by the Bulkhead Saloon, with lead-bordered colored glass in the orifice of each swinging door. It was famous for its free lunch of "Bull's Head Stew"; a neighboring saloon competed by serving "Cannibal Sandwiches": slices of pumpernickel with raw hamburger and a slice of onion on top.

Even the sailors had changed. Under the guidance of Furuseth and following his example, they started to take pride in their work. They developed a feeling of camaraderie; officers often mingled with the crew in saloons, and treated them with respect aboard ship. They all participated in parades, hundreds marching with their heads held high, everyone dressed alike in the union's white shirt, blue cap and trousers.

The Sailors' Union of the Pacific now had its headquarters on the second floor of the Audiffred Building. From the window of his office, Furuseth looked down on East Street and the Mission Street Wharf. He could see the Ferry Building, the ferry boats plying the bay, and the ships coming south past the Ferry Building to dock at the several wharves at this end of the waterfront.

Furuseth had moved his living quarters from 32 Steuart Street to a boardinghouse at 106 Steuart, known as Johnny Walker's place, across the street from the Audiffred Building.

In the first year of the new century, the maritime unions were growing rapidly. There were now 15 to 20 individual unions: sailors, longshoremen, teamsters, mates, engineers, marine firemen, marine cooks and stewards. Furuseth saw that this many different groups invited trouble. He was concerned that younger and less experienced unions might call premature strikes or make unreasonable demands upon the shipowners, which might precipitate a fight that could put all of the waterfront workers out of work. So he threw his prestige and energy behind the newly formed City Front Federation, a consolidation of all waterfront unions.

Employers in San Francisco became concerned over the threat posed by the growing strength of unions. In April 1901, fifty of them met secretly to revitalize the Employers' Association, pledged to eradicate the unions and to make San Francisco an "open shop" city. The Association, whose membership remained a secret, operated through sub-associations in each industry, all directed by an attorney, M.F. Michael, the only individual publicly identified with the secret group.

The Association intended to break one union at a time, and started with the uptown unions. When the metal polishers went on strike, many employers were willing to settle with the union, but they were informed that any firm that signed an agreement would have its supplies cut off. The Metal Polishers Union gave in. When the cooks and waiters struck for better working conditions, the restaurant owners who signed with the union found their oyster and meat supplies cut off. Any retail butcher who displayed a union shop card in his window could no longer get meat from the wholesalers. The clash between the employers and labor came to a head in July when 6,400 teamsters were locked out for refusing to haul nonunion baggage. It became clear that the employers intended to bust all the unions, one by one. So, the City Front Federation, representing 15,000 waterfront workers, voted to support the teamsters. Consternation! The port of San Francisco was closed, and half of the business in the city came to a halt.

The City Front Federation selected Furuseth as strike manager. Politically, he represented the most powerful union on the waterfront, employers respected him as a fair-minded and levelheaded union leader, and the workers knew and trusted him.

Furuseth went quietly to all those he knew with influence

among the employers, urging them to take steps to prevent open warfare. Mayor James D. Phelan offered to act as arbitrator, but Michael said the employers had nothing to arbitrate and refused even to meet with union representatives. The business elements were well organized and had strong political connections. They hired scabs and then demanded, and got, additional police to ride on the wagons driven by scab teamsters. Many of the special police were ex-convicts, prize fighters, and professional strikebreakers. Inevitably, violence erupted, men on both sides were beaten, and the waterfront once again was stained with blood.

On Labor Day of 1901, over 20,000 unionists marched in a four-mile parade that took two hours to pass in close formation. With Furuseth in the lead, the sailors marched proudly, all sharply attired in their dress uniforms. Later, Furuseth addressed the strikers, pleading with them not to be provoked by the strikebreakers, and encouraging them to stand fast in the strike.

But, after ten weeks of bitter conflict, labor came to the conclusion that it could not win; the Employers' Association was too strong. Furuseth had been beaten by superior forces, but he had acted as a competent leader. He would be ready to do battle again at a more opportune time. "Tomorrow is also a day."

Governor Henry T. Gage announced a settlement of the strike, although no details of the agreement were ever revealed. Five men had been killed, and 336 wounded. But the Strike of 1901 had not been a complete defeat. Furuseth's Sailors' Union of the Pacific had gained nothing for itself, but the secret Michael group had failed to bust the unions, it had failed to establish San Francisco as an "open shop" city.

Labor learned a lesson from the City Front strike. The employers controlled both the Republican and the Democratic political organizations, and so also had full control of the city government, including the police department and the mayor's office. So, after the strike a Union Labor Party was organized in San Francisco. At first, Furuseth, following his belief that unions should operate only through the two established political parties, called it "a sad mistake." But later—in one of the few times in his life when he changed his mind—he saw the necessity of an independent political party. It was needed in order to take control of the city government out of the hands of the Employers' Association. In October, the *Coast Seamen's Journal* came out in full support of the Union Labor Party candidate. Labor's victory in the following city election encouraged further political activity.

A move was initiated to draft Furuseth to run for the United States Congress. His salary was then 30 dollars a month, or 360 dollars a year. A congressman received 5,000 dollars. Did that influence him? Not one bit. He had seen enough of Washington. There were a few good and honest men in Congress, but he had seen what the thirst for power and wealth did to many. They would pledge support for something that might help the sailor—then switch positions easy enough if it became to the congressman's personal or political advantage to do so. Furuseth believed he could help his sailors only if he wanted nothing for himself.

"But, Andy," someone said. "A congressman gets 5,000 dollars. Don't you want the money?"

"No," he replied. "I don't want any more than I have. A man who owns too many possessions wants to hang on to them. So he is often tempted to compromise in order to keep what he has."

Furuseth refused to compromise. There were times when he could have obtained all he sought for his deck sailors, if he would do so at the expense of the marine firemen, or if he would accept less adequate provisions for the safety of the travelling public. But he refused to barter the interests of one class at the expense of the other. Rather than compromise upon the halfway measure, he would accept delay and disappointment, confident that "tomorrow is also a day." Now, he preferred to keep his roots in the labor movement, where he could live without the necessity of compromising what he believed in. So, despite pleas, he refused to be drafted for political office.

Some people called Furuseth resolute and steadfast; others called him stubborn and mule-headed. They all agreed that when he determined in his own mind what was right, or what was wrong, nothing could budge him from his convictions. He didn't think something; he *knew* it. He had many fixed ideas, and they all seemed to have been generated from the core of his philosophy: the words, the quotation he had cross-stitched on the piece of white linen cloth.

For the next four years after the City Front strike, the sailors and shipowners had a comparatively friendly relationship. One of the reasons was that Furuseth insisted that the union make no unreasonable demands on the owners. When he thought the union was in the wrong, he said so. Also, he believed that the best way for the shipowners to reduce operating expenses was not to lower wages but to hire more efficient crews. And it was the union's duty to increase the sailors' skill and responsibility, to eliminate drunks and loafers, and to supply competent crews.

By the winter of 1905, however, the cost of living had risen to new heights and the sailors would no longer accept the old wage rates. After prolonged negotiations and before the issue could be settled, an event occurred that disrupted not only the negotiations, but the entire city.

At 5:12 a.m. on Wednesday, April 18, 1906, the earth

suddenly shifted for 300 miles along the ancient San Andreas fault which passes under San Francisco. The release of a mighty pent-up energy shook the city violently. The pavement pulsated and swayed like a living thing, buildings collapsed, deep fissures opened up on Van Ness Avenue, streetcar tracks on Market Street twisted into snakes, the man-made land over old Yerba Buena Cove slumped, columns of the City Hall buckled and the great dome crashed to the ground.

This all happened in less than two minutes.

Then hissing, broken gas jets were ignited by electrical sparks, producing instant flashes of red. The city burst into flames!

The fires lasted for four days.

The sounds of anguish rose everywhere; frenzied horses stampeded through narrow streets; people rushed to escape the flames. A series of aftershocks intensified the panic. Water mains had been broken by the quake. No water! Fires, all over the city, were out of control. The heat was so intense that wooden frame houses burst into flames even before the wall of fire reached them.

Without water, the only weapon left was dynamite. Soldiers from the Presidio and the city firemen set off charges the length of Van Ness Avenue, trying to halt the westward spread of flames at this line. Dynamite was detonated in other sections of the city, with the hope of stopping the spreading flames.

When the fires were finally brought under control, four square miles of San Francisco had been devastated—over 500 city blocks—28,000 buildings were destroyed, and 25,000 people had been left homeless. Those people who were killed directly numbered 498. The indirect casualties—those who died within a year from suicide, injuries, or disease—brought the total fatalities to 3,000.

Most of the waterfront lay flat and burned out. But there were a few surprises. It is said that Hippolite d' Audiffred, the Frenchman, went down to the waterfront to survey the damage. He stopped with a jerk, and gasped in astonishment at the sight before him: nothing but a broad expanse of gray ashes, with smoke rising. And there, standing alone and with just a few bricks missing, was his Audiffred Building! It alone had survived!

The mystery was solved when he talked to the bartender of the Bulkhead Saloon, his ground floor tenant. It seems that as soldiers and firemen approached the building to blow it up, the saloonkeeper offered to make a bargain: two quarts of whiskey for each firefighter and a firehouse cart full of wine, if they would spare the building. So, the Audiffred Building survived the earthquake and fire of 1906. (And it is still standing today.)

Over in the battered business district, surrounded by still smoking ruins, the Hotaling warehouse, stocked with whiskey, also remained unharmed. This caused someone to compose a jingle:

If, as they say, God struck the town
For being over-frisky,
Why did He burn all the churches down
But spare Hotaling's whiskey?

Furuseth was in Washington at the time of the fire and earthquake. When he returned to San Francisco, he found the headquarters of the SUP still intact on the second floor of the Audiffred Building, but his boarding house was just a pile of ashes. At the far end of Market Street, near the base of Twin Peaks, there was a neighborhood inhabited mostly by Scandinavians. Furuseth found a private home at 59 Beaver Street, rented a room, and used it as his residence for the few months of each year that he was in San Francisco.

The city bustled with frenzied activity. Spirited citizens and hired help cleared away the mass of debris, and new buildings sprang up with unbelievable speed. Hotels, restaurants, offices, shops, homes—almost always more fine and luxurious than before. Not a single house, shabby or otherwise, remained in the devastated area. Merchants rushed to get their share of the new booming business opportunities. Prices shot up, and wages raced after prices in an upward dizzying spiral . . . But not the wages of the sailors.

Furuseth tried to reopen the negotiations that had been disrupted by the earthquake and fire. He sought a five dollar per month raise. The shipowners refused; they had joined the United Shipping and Transportation Association and had posted bonds of 60,000 dollars to pledge that no member would raise wages without the consent of the Association's executive board.

In desperation, the seamen, the cooks and stewards, and the firemen went on strike, electing Furuseth as strike manager. Once again, he used the "Oracle," putting aboard a vessel a dummy crew that would jump ship at the last minute. When the owners started to import scabs from Chicago, Mexico, Hawaii, and Australia, the union sent a launch to meet all incoming vessels for the purpose of convincing the scabs—by argument, if possible; and by force, if necessary—to desert nonunion ships.

The shipowners fought back with more potent weapons. They arranged through the mayor's office to get 50 special police assigned to the waterfront. In San Francisco, a striking seaman was shot dead. In Aberdeen, a gunman hired by the Shipowners' Association murdered a union member in a barroom fight. The owners also used the courts, securing a number of injunctions to enjoin the union and its officials from interfering with their ships.

Furuseth had studied intensely the history of injunctions and had read numerous court decisions. The injunction was a form of equity, a remedy the courts could use to rectify situations not covered by law. But, Furuseth argued, it was never meant to be applied to labor; the courts could use it only to protect property or property rights. And "labor is not property," he argued. "The fundamental principle of American law is that there shall be no property rights in man. A man's labor power is part of him; it fluctuates with his health, decreases when he grows old, and ceases at his death. It cannot be divorced from man, and therefore, under our system, cannot be property."

Furuseth felt strongly that the use of the injunction in labor disputes was an illegal usurpation of power by the courts which, if allowed to continue, would bring an end to liberty. His life was dedicated to securing freedom for the sailor, to foster and retain individual liberty. Injunctions in labor disputes would destroy that liberty, so Furuseth advised his men to disobey injunctions. Defiance of such orders might result in being sent to jail, but he contended that there was no disgrace in going to jail. "The disgrace comes from the reason one is sent there."

Once, when he had defied an injunction, Furuseth was confronted with the possibility of serving a jail sentence. His reply has become a classic in American labor history. Speaking slowly, with his Norwegian accent, he replied, "You can put me in jail, but you cannot give me narrower quarters than as a seaman I have always had. You cannot give me coarser food than I have always eaten. You cannot make me lonelier than I have always been."

Chapter Six

In 1909, when Furuseth was 55 years old, his brown hair was still parted on the right side, but a tinge of white now appeared around the edges. His face was no longer plump, and age had brought tiny wrinkles to his cheeks and around his lips. But his hazel eyes had not changed; they still stared straight ahead with a now famous look of determination.

Since 1900, his stature had grown in the labor movement. As the leader of two important strikes on the West Coast in 1901 and 1906, he was the best known labor leader on the coast. The year before, the AFL had rewarded Furuseth for his faithful service by electing him to represent the American labor movement in the British Trade Union Congress in Nottingham, England, and he also attended a convention of the International Transport Workers in Vienna on behalf of the ISU. While there, he pleaded that seamen should be treated as free men, but found little sympathy for his cause among the European delegates. "They do not seem to feel the chains," he said. "It does not seem as if the men are really conscious of their serfdom." He concluded that everywhere in Europe the workers were under the influence of the socialists. And he was unalterably convinced that the socialists were looking, not for freedom, but for government control and the destruction of individualism.

Because of his widespread activities, Furuseth had many associates and acquaintances, but he had only a few friends.

He had a dignity and aloofness that discouraged intimacy. He knew countless sailors on the West Coast and all over the country. He knew them as sailors, as union members, and he allowed them to know him only in the same way. One of the old-timers explained, "Furuseth was a great man, did a lot for us sailors. But we didn't get to know him. He was a big shot, was president of the International. Oh, we liked him a lot. But we never got close to him, if you know what I mean."

His associate leaders in the union were primarily white-collar former sailors and conservatives like Walter Macarthur, Paul Scharrenberg, and Victor Olander, all of whom were his friends. At AFL headquarters, he was on cordial terms with Samuel Gompers and John Frey, but with no others. He was well acquainted with many shipowners, and, despite their battles, he was respected by them for his honesty and fairness. Newspapermen, including William Randolph Hearst and Fremont Older of the *San Francisco Bulletin*, praised him for his sincerity, honesty, and reliability. In Washington, many congressmen respected him for his ability to stand up against the best maritime lawyers the shipowners could hire. Attorneys Silas Axtell and Hutton of California were trusted friends. A mutual friendship developed between Justice Brandeis of the Supreme Court, who occasionally invited Furuseth to spend an evening in his home.

In 1909, Furuseth met another national figure, and this time it proved to be a turning point in his life. Senator Robert La Follette became what might rightly be described as the closest friend of the loner. Bob La Follette was his soul mate, the man who would help him to ultimately reach the goal he had so long yearned for.

La Follette was born in 1855 in a log cabin at Primrose, Wisconsin. As a boy on the farm, he felt the Granger movement "swirling" about him. The plight of the farmers, and the arrogant power of the railroad moguls, made a lasting impression. While a student at the University of Wisconsin he was profoundly influenced by a great teacher, President John Bascom, who inspired him with a deep sense of the obligations of citizenship. He became a lawyer, and was then elected district attorney despite opposition from the powerful local boss of his own Republican party. Two years later, he again defied the political machine and was elected to the House of Representatives. After serving three terms he was defeated by the Democratic landslide of 1890 and returned to the practice of law. Next, he served as governor of Wisconsin from 1900 to 1905, promoting laws to regulate the railroads and to reform taxes. In 1906, he was elected to the U.S. Senate as a Republican, but he steadfastly pursued an independent policy on legislation, which drew the scorn of Republican "Old Guard" senators. He founded *La Follette's Magazine*, and year after year used it in his educational campaign to help the farmers and other common people, and to fight the railroad corporations and the powerful investment bankers.

The meeting of Furuseth and La Follette came about partly because Furuseth also thought and acted as an individual, guided by his conscience.

Furuseth had given his belated blessing to the Union Labor Party in San Francisco after the failure of the 1901 strike. The victorious party had elected Eugene Schmitz as mayor of San Francisco. But now it became apparent that Schmitz was a mere figurehead, that the city was actually governed by Abraham Ruef, and that Boss Ruef was a crook.

Furuseth learned, through his friend Fremont Older, crusading editor of the *San Francisco Bulletin*, that Boss Ruef and the San Francisco Board of Supervisors had received hundreds of thousands of dollars as bribes for granting an overhead trolley franchise. Ruef, or at least his lieutenants, maintained houses of ill fame; he arranged city contracts for his friends, and pocketed huge amounts of money. Furuseth knew that disclosures of widespread corruption would eventually be made, and he wanted a clean break with the Union Labor Party so that labor could disassociate itself from these coming scandals.

When Charles M. Fickert, the Union Labor Party candidate, ran for district attorney against Francis J. Heney (supported by Fremont Older), Furuseth declared his support for Heney. For this he was branded a "scab" and a "traitor to labor." Once again, he fought for what he believed to be right, and attacked what he believed to be wrong, with never any thought of how his action might affect his own position. When Fickert won the election, Furuseth deplored the victory of the Union Labor Party as a victory for dishonesty, graft, and corruption. His courageous stand on an unpopular position lost him the support of many labor people.

On the other hand, he received an unexpected benefit. The defeated candidate, Francis Heney, knew someone in Washington who Furuseth should meet. True, he was a Republican, but he was a good one, a Progressive Republican. The next time Furuseth went to Washington, he held in his hand a letter of introduction from Heney to Senator Robert M. La Follette of Wisconsin.

Years later, La Follette described their first meeting in December of 1909. He drew a vivid picture of the "tall, bony, slightly stooped man, with a face bespeaking superior intelligence and lofty character, who called that day because he wanted to interest me in the cause of the American sailor. He was a sailor himself, he said, and he wanted to 'be free.' I did not know what he meant. I questioned him. Surely there were no slaves under the American flag. Bondsmen there were—but Lincoln changed all that. And it had been written in the amended Constitution.

"'Yes,' he said, 'but not for the sailor. All other men are free. But when the amendments were framed, they passed us by. The sailor was forgotten.'

"I asked him to tell me about it. Sitting on the edge of the chair, his body thrust forward, a great soul speaking through his face, the set purpose of his life shining in his eyes, he told me the story of the sailor's wrongs. He said little of himself, excepting as I drew him on to speak of the long, long struggle of which he was the beginning . . . He spoke with a strong Scandinavian accent, but with remarkable facility of expression, force and discrimination.

"He knew the maritime law of every country; the social condition, the wage level, the economic life of each sea-faring nation. He was master of his subject . . . He was logical, rugged, terse, quaint, and fervid with conviction."

La Follette was so moved and impressed that he invited Furuseth to come to his home the following Sunday morning for breakfast. Furuseth did, and for the next few years he went to the La Follette home almost every Sunday for breakfast. He came as close to leading a family life at those breakfasts as he ever did in his entire life.

La Follette saw that Furuseth's sailors needed help as much as did his own farmers. He offered that he and Furuseth together would make the sailor free.

Up to that time, the Maguire Acts and the White Act had been of some help, but most of the fundamental problems still remained. Furuseth had tried to get two more bills passed, but Congress, dominated by standpat Republicans and persuaded by the shipowners' lobby, ignored the seamen's proposals. None of them even reached the floor for debate. In fact, Furuseth had to fight to guard the gains already made in the Maguire and White Acts against attempts to whittle them down.

Now, with the encouragement of his friend La Follette, Furuseth put together a proposed, comprehensive bill that ultimately covered 20 needed reforms. Some related to improved working conditions, such as an increase in the forecastle space, better food, and such.

Others pertained to safety measures. With the change from sail to steam, the skilled sailor found that he could be, and was, replaced by cheap unskilled labor. Furuseth argued that even if unskilled men could handle the work aboard a steamship, experienced seamen were needed in times of emergency, men who knew how to lower lifeboats in a heavy sea, and knew how to protect the lives of passengers. He proposed that 65 per cent of the deck crew of all vessels be able-bodied seamen. For similar reasons, he also proposed that 75 per cent of the crew must be able to understand any order given by an officer; in other words, on American ships they must be able to speak English so they could act effectively in times of emergency. Furuseth sincerely believed in these "safety of the seas" proposals. Of course, the fact that most of these unskilled laborers were Chinese, and that they worked for one-quarter of union scale, was an additional evil he hoped to correct.

There was also a provision controlling the payment of advances or allotments in such a way that more of the wages would go directly to the sailors instead of first passing through the sticky fingers of the crimps.

But the cornerstone of the proposed bill, its most outstanding feature, was the requirement that the United States abrogate all treaties providing for the arrest, detention, and return of foreign seamen deserting in an American port. Any seaman coming to America should be free to leave his ship. This would enable sailors to fight their economic battles equipped with the same legal right to quit work that free men ashore possess. If a foreign seaman could desert in American ports, foreign shipowners would be forced to hire crews in those ports at American wage scales, or they would have to pay the same rates to their foreign crews to keep them from deserting. This would keep wages from falling to the lowest level.

And the bill also provided that all other provisions in the proposed legislation would be made applicable to foreign ships in American harbors. For example, a British vessel carrying a Chinese crew who couldn't understand an English order would be denied clearance from an American port. The British would thus be forced to hire crews meeting American standards if they wanted to trade with the United States.

Senator La Follette introduced the bill in 1910, but the opposition was so powerful that he couldn't force action on it. Furuseth was bitter, and vowed to continue the fight "even though the consummation be deferred for a thousand tomorrows."

The following year, La Follette introduced it again in the Senate, and Congressman Wilson introduced the same bill in the House. The shipowners opposed them.

In the midst of the controversy, an iceberg sank the "unsinkable" *Titanic* with a loss of 1,513 lives. Only a few days before the tragedy, Furuseth had written to the House Committee pointing out the need for more lifeboats and enough qualified men to man them. Except for the lack of these, not one life would have been lost in the *Titanic* disaster. After a public outcry, the opposition could no longer ignore the bills, although it took another eight months to pass both Houses. By that time it had been so watered down that Furuseth and La Follette were almost relieved when President Taft pocket vetoed the bill, for the reason that it might "create friction with the commerce of foreign nations."

Now Furuseth would have to start all over, this time with a new Congress and a new president: Woodrow Wilson. He began by sending the President an eight-page typewritten analysis of the La Follette bill. Again, Congress dragged its feet. More delays.

After a series of complicated parliamentary maneuvers, La Follette finally got the bill to the Senate floor for final hearing. The lobby opposing the bill was on hand in force, and telegrams were pouring in from boards of trade, big shippers, and chambers of commerce. Senators were bombarded with pleas to delay action.

At the hearing, La Follette analyzed the bill, then went into an impassioned plea. The day before, the *Volturno* had burned and sank off the coast of Newfoundland, and 136 passengers had drowned. The loss of life was due largely to the lack of efficient men to handle the lifeboats—only eight able seamen on board. La Follette vividly described what was necessary to lower a lifeboat during an emergency. Then he pointed to Furuseth in the gallery. He referred to Furuseth as "one of the most intelligent men it has ever been my good fortune to meet . . . For 19 years he has been sitting up there in that corner of the gallery waiting to be made free. Whatever I happen to know about this subject I have acquired from talking with him." La Follette pleaded for the emancipation of the sailors from serfdom and for the safety of human life at sea. "We now come," he declared, "to another test of corporate power arrayed against human rights. What shall it be?"

Late in the afternoon of October 23, 1913, the La Follette Seamen's Bill was agreed to without a roll call vote.

The bill had passed.

Furuseth sprang out of the gallery into the upper corridor, crying out, "This finishes the work Lincoln began." Tears were running down his cheeks. He put his hands to his throat, saying, "I am choking, I am so happy."

But the battle was not yet won. The bill still had to pass the House. The shipowners raised such strong protests that the House Committee consented to additional testimony and more delays. Furuseth talked to congressmen with passion, and wrote many letters, pleading for passage of the bill.

Once again, a ship sank—and gave him providential ammunition. This time it was the *Empress of Ireland* on the St. Lawrence River with a tragic loss of 1,026 lives.

But months passed by, and nothing happened.

Fifteen months after the Senate passed the Seamen's Bill, it was finally reported out of the Conference Committee of the House. But now only a few critical days remained before Congress automatically adjourned. Unless passed by both Houses and signed by the President before noon on March 4, 1915, the bill would die. Furuseth would have to begin his long fight all over again.

The House approved the conference report without a recorded vote, but there was strong opposition in the Senate. Once again, La Follette displayed his parliamentary skills. Among other things, he managed to have a vote taken when his main opponents were temporarily out of the Senate chamber.

The bill passed.

Now all that was left was the uncertain task of getting President Wilson's signature.

La Follette and Furuseth knew that Wilson favored the humanitarian aspects of the legislation, but also knew there were good reasons why the President might not sign the bill. Great Britain, Germany, and other nations had filed protests against the measure. The United States had commercial treaties with 22 nations which provided for the arrest, detention, and return of seamen who deserted. Wilson might be persuaded that the enactment of the Seamen's Bill could disturb existing treaties and cause disorder in our commercial relations, with grave consequences.

Through the President's secretary, Joseph P. Tumulty, La Follette was granted an appointment with Wilson. Although the appointment had been requested only for himself, he decided to take Furuseth with him. That evening, La Follette talked with Wilson for 15 minutes, and then Furuseth was called into the room. He probably knew he had only a few minutes to present his case, and in those few minutes 20 years of work might be done or undone. If the President refused to sign now, the Seamen's Bill was killed . . . perhaps forever. It was now or never.

When they left, President Wilson telephoned his secretary. "Tumulty, I have just experienced a great half-hour, the tensest since I came to the White House." He later explained that Furuseth had held him spellbound with the power of his speech and argument.

When Furuseth was asked years later what happened that night, he replied, "I can't remember what I said or did. That doesn't matter. It was La Follette's job. I was very much stirred up. I was all aflame . . . The President asked me some questions and I answered them. There were tears in La Follette's eyes. He was awfully moved... Then I was dismissed from the room."

But March 4 was drawing near, and the President had still not made up his mind. March 2, no news. March 3, no news. The morning of March 4 arrived. Only a few hours remained before Congress would adjourn. An hour before adjournment, Furuseth learned that President Wilson had signed the bill! The La Follette Seamen's Act was law!

The President explained, "I debated the matter of signing the bill very earnestly indeed ... and finally determined to sign it because it seemed the only chance to get something like justice to a class of workmen who have been too much neglected by our laws."

La Follette was overjoyed for his own personal achievement, for his friend Furuseth, and for what they had done for the seamen of the world.

We can imagine how Furuseth felt.

After over 25 years in the labor movement, he had finally achieved what he had set out to do. He had reached the high point in his career. He began to be called the "Abraham Lincoln of the Sea."

But even now, Furuseth avoided personal publicity, even refused to have his photograph taken. This reluctance was explained by Victor Olander, who was the secretary-treasurer of the Illinois State Federation of Labor:

"(Many years ago) one of the Boston newspapers offered Furuseth the use of very liberal space for convention publicity if he would permit the publication of his photograph. Andy came to me about it.

"'What shall I do, Vic? They offer to let me say whatever I want to say.' He was sorely troubled.

"'Why let them photograph you, of course,' said I. 'You can't refuse the opportunity offered to put the story of the seamen before the public through such a widely read paper.'

"But Andy shook his head, not as though he was refusing anything, but rather as though he were giving up—sadly and with doubt and hesitation—something of great value.

"'I'm afraid I can't,' he said.

"'Why not?' I demanded. 'What's so precious about that face of yours that it may not appear in a newspaper?'

"His attitude was not new to me. Others had ridiculed his seeming sensitiveness about being photographed—some even sneered—but I knew the man too well to have anything but respect for his feelings. Yet at that time I pressed him hard. Finally he told me that he feared the injection of his own personality into the publicity relating to the struggle of the seamen would make the fight appear too much like that of one man, whereas it was really the struggle of thousands, and that this might make it more difficult to secure the legislation we were seeking . . .

"'I don't want to let them publish my picture until the seamen's bill is enacted—then they can do what they please with both me and my face.'

"He spoke in a very positive tone, with just a touch of bitterness. It seemed as though he had taken a vow.

"I suddenly sensed his difficulty. Up to that time he had worked very much alone. Only a few understood the fundamentals of the freedom which he was seeking for the men of the sea. He had worked alone, lived alone, fought alone—with little understanding on the part of even the membership of our union.

"It was his fight, and he knew it. But to all the world he proposed to show the seamen themselves fighting, and so he struggled along for all of them. Do I make my meaning clear? That's Furuseth. He would not be photographed."

Now, with the passage of the Seamen's Act, but only as a favor to his friend La Follette, he finally consented to have his picture taken.

La Follette once wrote that Furuseth conducted himself so inconspicuously and humbly " . . . that the public had little opportunity to know the man. Even the measure that represents his great life work, the Seamen's Act, bears, by Congressional usage, not the name of Furuseth; but of—La Follette."

It is ironic that in later years when Furuseth was beaten down and needed support, his plea for recognition would be denied. And it is sad that after all the disheartening years of the long fight to secure the seamen's freedom, he would have to struggle the rest of his life to prevent that freedom from being taken away again.

His adversaries were many, and they continued to come at him from all directions. But his whole personality cried out for justice that would not be denied. He was to be beaten again and again, each defeat only stimulating him to fight harder.

Chapter Seven

Back in San Francisco, the Sailors' Union of the Pacific moved its headquarters from the Audiffred Building to 57 Clay Street, just half a block up from the Embarcadero (as East Street was now called). But for two years, Furuseth was seldom there. The shipowners, outraged at the passage of the Seamen's Act, denounced it with dire predictions of the serious complications its enactment would produce. Together with the chambers of commerce, they enlisted all their political power to find ways to emasculate the provisions in the Act. So serious did Furuseth consider the attacks on the law that for two years he seldom left Washington.

To answer the shipowners' charges, Furuseth wrote articles and he spoke to any group that would listen. He offered to debate the shipowners, but none would accept the challenge. He declared that Congress had followed the advice of the shipowners for 150 years, as a result of which the United States had practically no American merchant marine. He pleaded that the Seamen's Act be given a fair trial.

The shipowners had other plans. Having failed with Congress and the President, they turned to an agency with which they had more influence: the Department of Commerce. It had the duty to administer the law and to interpret its provisions. But whenever the Department was asked to interpret the Seamen's Act, the decision was almost always in favor of the shipowners.

Robert Dollar and the Pacific Mail Steamship Company, among others, operated with all-Chinese crews and white officers. The law provided that 75 per cent of the crew had to be able to understand the language of the officers. The Department interpreted this to mean that pidgin English and sign language would suffice—certainly not the intent of the law nor what Furuseth had envisioned.

The law required that at least 65 per cent of the deck crew be able-bodied seamen. In order to create the impression that the Seamen's Act was impractical because there were not enough qualified able seamen available, the Department interpreted the physical examination required for an A.B. certificate so strictly that mere color blindness or a missing finger would disqualify a man—even those who had sailed for 20 or 30 years. (Furuseth did succeed in getting this one requirement modified.)

Furuseth tried hard to get favorable decisions out of Commerce, but most were equally one-sided. Frustrated at every turn, he said, in disgust, "There does not appear to be anything that can be done with the Department."

But he wouldn't give up. He would find another way. He had to change tack, had to set a new course of action.

"The owners are loud in their demands that the laws shall be obeyed by someone else," he said. "Perhaps the laws were only intended to be obeyed by the sailors and not by the owners. But we shall see."

He turned to the law courts. Furuseth had no trained legal advisors available, so he sought free legal advice at the Legal Aid Society at One Broadway, in New York City. There he met Silas Axtell, who had just recently been admitted to practice law and who had his first job as attorney for the Seamen's Branch of the Legal Aid Society. He had already seen some of the disabilities and infirmities from which the seamen suffered. It was a stroke of good fortune that the two men met, because Axtell became not only Furuseth's legal advisor, but also his trusted and lifelong friend. Axtell, together with a couple of other attorneys—including Gilbert Roe, an associate of La Follette's—handled all the Seamen's Act cases that were to come to court over a period of several years.

Furuseth was not a silent or passive client. A great deal of correspondence passed between the two men, Axtell writing from his office in New York City, and Furuseth from his small attic room in the National Hotel in Washington. The self-assured old warrior considered himself at least an equal to the attorney in suggesting the cases to be tried, the precedents to be followed, and even the line of argument to be used.

Furuseth insisted on being kept advised. We find a letter from Axtell in response to Furuseth's request for a status report on 11 pending cases. We find such reports as:

"RONLAND, et al. vs. STRATHEARN, appeal and bond for costs filed; copy of minutes received; minutes sent back to Nelson & Laird, local attorneys, at Pensacola, Fla., with instructions to have same printed. Can get the brief out in twenty-four hours. Case will probably be reached for argument in June."

"FERNANDEZ vs. STANDARD OIL CO. OF NEW JERSEY. Suit brought for seaman whose wrist was broken through negligent order of the mate transmitted through the boatswain. Tried before Judge Augustus Hand. Held that Sec. 20 abolished only defense of the defendant. Case properly sent to the jury. Verdict $7500. Rather than stand an appeal plaintiff settled for $5750.00"

Axtell ended his letter with, "I trust that this report will be satisfactory, but if it is not please advise, and I will try to oblige you."

The *Arago* case, in which the court upheld the imprison-

THE ABRAHAM LINCOLN OF THE SEA

ment of sailors for "desertion" because the 13th Amendment didn't apply to seamen, had been one of Furuseth's most bitter disappointments. It must have been with satisfaction that he read this report which was reminiscent of *Arago*:

"LARSEN vs. CALAO: This is an action where a seaman was taken off the ship by order of the Consul at Valparaiso, at the instigation of the master. He was kept in jail for four or five days, and left in the port. This was the case where the master was acting without authority and justification. We brought action in rem, which is pending, but I am also bringing action against the owners personally at common law."

Even the buckoes were no longer getting away with their brutality:

"JOHNSON vs. BELMONT: This is a case of assault and unlawful punishment by the master and officers, to a member of the crew. The owners are settling the case for a substantial sum, which is a good victory."

Furuseth not only wanted to know the status of all cases, but he didn't hesitate to interject himself into them—perhaps the most irksome irritation that an attorney can be subjected to. For example, he wrote Axtell, "It seems to me that we should bend every energy to get those cases decided our way and as speedy as possible.... Those two cases now assume a very much enlarged importance and I suggest that you invite Mr. Gilbert E. Roe to assist you in these cases. I am writing to him within the next few days to ask that he co-operate with you ... "

A sensitive lawyer might resent this obtrusiveness— might even want to get rid of Furuseth as a client—but Axtell understood and admired him. He said of Furuseth, "Certainly he was no average man. He was a most unusual and uncommon man. An ascetic by temperament, and intensely religious. Dominated by a spirit of selflessness, he effaced himself from every undertaking but struggled with every legitimate means to accomplish his purpose. . . . Furuseth was great because he eliminated himself. He sought no reward of a material character. He sought no publicity, no fame, no reputation. He was great because he asked no thanks. He was great because he was a son of God who lived as the brother of all men and devoted all his mind and heart to the service of others."

Over 30 Seamen's Act cases had been tried or were pending when suddenly the whole picture changed. Congress declared war on Germany on April 6, 1917. The Seamen's Act was virtually suspended for the duration of the conflict.

When World War I began in 1914, it had a far-reaching effect on seamen. At first, before the entry of the U.S., there were apparent benefits for them. Foreign shipowners began to hire large numbers of American sailors, a sudden shortage of qualified men developed, and wages rose. Seamen began to flock into the union, raising the membership of the ISU from 16,000 to 30,000.

But years later the aftermath of the war would prove to be disastrous for the seafarers.

Furuseth opposed the U.S. entry into the war from the beginning, as did the unions and most of the public. "The sentiment of the working people of the U.S. is," he said, "overwhelmingly in favor of peace and against war . . . Each man's life is his own and he will ultimately be guided by the sentiment that is in him."

He bore the Germans no personal ill will, and in response to proposals by the unions of allied nations that seamen pledge themselves not to sail with German seamen, Furuseth refused to condemn the German sailors.

"Hatred once developed does not cease with the war" he said, "and it will then be used by the shipowners to pit seamen against seamen in the economic struggle."

When a German submarine sank the British liner *Lusitania* with the loss of 1,198 lives, we can be sure Furuseth abhored the cowardly attack on an unarmed merchant vessel. But he put much of the blame on the shipowners, who sent the ship out improperly manned with an inefficient crew, fully loaded with both passengers and a cargo including munitions, and in defiance of German warnings.

Senator La Follette introduced resolutions calling upon President Wilson to assemble all neutral nations for the purpose of halting the European war. He argued that the nation's entire economy was dominated by fewer than 100 men who were, in turn, controlled by J.P. Morgan and Standard Oil investment banking groups. Concerned that the U.S. was about to be dragged into the war by the business interests to protect their investments, La Follette became a leader of the opposition.

Furuseth wholeheartedly agreed with his friend's proposals, and urged the labor movement to support them.

President Wilson, having proclaimed the neutrality of the United States in August 1914, strove to maintain it and to be impartial. He tried every way he could to get the belligerents to accept U.S. mediation, but failed. When the Germans announced they would resume unrestricted submarine warfare, Wilson severed diplomatic relations with Germany on February 3, 1917.

But the U.S. was still not ready for war. Public opinion was swung over to a more hostile mood by the publication of the Zimmerman Telegram.

At that time, Mexico was not on friendly terms with the United States, and one of its officials hinted to the Germans that they might be permitted to use the Mexican coast as bases for their submarines. Arthur Zimmerman, Germany's Secretary of Foreign Affairs, sent a coded telegram to his ambassador in Mexico, instructing him to make a proposal: If the United States should enter the war against Germany, and if Mexico should become Germany's ally, Mexico might thereby be able to recover Texas, New Mexico, and Arizona from the United States. The British Admiralty intelligence intercepted and decoded the message, and communicated it to Wilson on February 24. When published in the U.S. press, it set off a nationwide demand for war against Germany.

Wilson immediately asked Congress to take all measures to protect U.S. commerce—and more specifically, to arm all merchant vessels.

The American public, now revengeful and increasingly fueled by a wave of patriotism, clamored for war. Gompers and other labor leaders retreated from their previous isolation policy, and became enthusiastic supporters of a war policy they had once opposed.

But Furuseth refused to change. Both he and La Follette still stubbornly fought to keep America out of the war, convinced that it would be a catastrophe for the country.

The bill to provide for the arming of all merchant ships was before the Senate. La Follette was determined to defeat it, and saw his only hope lay in resorting to a filibuster. On the last day before adjournment, Furuseth was with La Follette in his office.

Furuseth paced back and forth, then suddenly turned and said in a tense voice, "Bob, if you defeat that bill, they'll crucify you."

La Follette replied, "I know it," and left for the Senate chamber.

Later in the day, the two met again. The Armed Ship Bill

had been defeated. "That bill meant war," La Follette said. "I had only two choices, to resign or defeat it."

Furuseth went over and put his arm around him (quite an uncharacteristic gesture for a Norwegian). "Bob," he said, "they'll crucify you. But God bless you."

And crucify him, they did. La Follette was denounced and burned in effigy. A few months later, he made an extemporaneous speech which was inaccurately quoted and grossly misrepresented in press reports from coast to coast. Some senators demanded his expulsion from the Senate. Others charged him with disloyalty and sedition. The feeling against La Follette didn't diminish until after the Armistice.

But La Follette never regretted his action nor did he retreat from his convictions.

Furuseth supported him throughout. But when the United States declared war on Germany on April 6, 1917, Furuseth realized that, despite his opposition to war, he had no choice but to fall in line. Although he bargained for as much as he could get for the seamen—union wages, war zone bonuses, and recognition of the union as their representative—he kept the demands and actions of organized seamen within reasonable bounds. Not an easy task, because prices rose much faster than wages.

Furuseth wrote *A Message To Seamen: A Call To The Sea*, in which he appealed to former seamen: "The nation that proclaimed your freedom now needs your services. America is at war. Our troops are being transported over the seas. Munitions and supplies are being shipped in ever increasing quantities to our armies in Europe . . . Thousands of skilled seamen, seafaring men of all capacities who left the sea in years gone by as a protest against serfdom from which no flag then offered relief, have now an opportunity to return to their former calling, sail as free men and serve our country."

The union consented to suspension of the able seamen's certificate requirement. And in what would later prove to have significant consequences, it agreed to cooperate in a recruitment and training program for merchant marine personnel. Furuseth asked the union members to show the new men how to become good seamen.

When the war ended, the ISU had increased its membership by 50 per cent over the prewar years. All the affiliated unions were stronger numerically and financially. But the war had changed the shipping industry, and some of the changes were not beneficial to the seamen.

During the war, the government actually tried to transfer the merchant marine to Navy control, which could have destroyed the unions. Furuseth had been able to block this move. But the government did manage to establish Sea Service Bureaus, or government hiring halls, to regulate employment. At the time, this seemed innocuous, but in later years the Bureau became the detested "fink hall."

The war decisively altered the character of the U.S. maritime industry. Between 1917 and 1922, the United States built 2,316 vessels—mostly steamships, although scores of large wooden schooners were also built in those years. The use of sailing ships was diminishing, however, and so also was the need for "real" sailors, those windship seamen who knew the special and difficult techniques needed to man a wind-propelled vessel. To be a crew member on a steamship required far less skill, and thousands of such men had been added to the labor market.

Furuseth once gave this travel advice to his union brothers: "If you can travel on the railroad, don't go on a ship. The kind of men that the shipowners have dug up from somewhere are of such an inefficient class that they could not do what is necessary for a seaman to do in hours of danger."

The full significance of these wartime changes, and the adverse impact they would have on seamen, would not be felt until 1921, three years after the Armistice.

During the interval, Furuseth had other battles to wage, this time on the international level. He turned his attention to the Peace Conference in Paris, suspecting that an international plot was afoot to destroy the Seamen's Act. There was talk about equalizing the standards for the merchant marine of all the countries in the world. This he feared would lower American standards. He went to Paris because, "(t)he question of the Peace Conference makes me shiver . . . There is where the seamen may be stripped of all hope."

The Peace Conference established the International Commission on Labor Legislation, which was not only approved by the leaders of the American Federation of Labor, but Samuel Gompers consented to be its chairman. Needless to say, Gompers was quite irritated when he learned that Furuseth later wrote to President Wilson denouncing the Gompers' committee as a plot to kill the American merchant marine.

The debate on labor's attitude toward the League of Nations took place at the AFL convention held in Atlantic City in June 1919. Furuseth suspected that international conferences dominated by governments and businessmen were out to harm his sailors. He was convinced that labor leaders in Europe and America were all wrong, and that only he was right. So, as a delegate, he opened the debate by saying, "It is a disagreeable job that I am now endeavoring to perform. I have struggled with myself for two months . . . There is something in me that ceaselessly, night and day, commands me to speak . . . It may be it will be stated that I am opposing here something that President Wilson wanted, and that my gratitude to him should be of such a nature as to keep my mouth shut . . . but my nature is such that I cannot follow blindly, no matter who it may be, and I cannot accept without protest the diluted labor propositions. "

He argued that Section 23 of the Covenant of the League of Nations established a superlegislature that would have almost unlimited power, and that Britain, with all the votes of its colonies and dominions, would control it. Furuseth objected not only to the substance of the proposal, but criticized several specific words and phrases, concluding that "there isn't a solitary thing here that leaves any of the American ideals in this document . . . I can't vote for this thing."

Furuseth received a tremendous ovation when he finished speaking. But then he was followed by top officials in the AFL, every one of whom disagreed with him. William Green of the United Mine Workers, while expressing his "profound regard" for Furuseth, stated that the proposition was not as bad as Furuseth thought. Samuel Gompers argued in favor of the League's covenant.

Of more than 30,000 votes cast, 99 per cent approved the committee report endorsing the League. Furuseth had lost.

He felt deeply the pain of rejection. He could avoid such pain if he would go along with the others, if he would compromise. But he felt that only he was looking out for the interests of the sailors. So, he had to do what he had done, had to do what he thought was right. Regardless of what others might think. Regardless of the consequences. Better to suffer rejection than to compromise.

By 1921, Furuseth's attention was drawn to another danger. The shipowners, with the connivance of the U.S. Shipping Board, were preparing a plan to smash the sailors' movement and to crush the unions. Sailors were now on three watches (that is, on an eight-hour day), for which they received 90 dollars a month and a dollar for overtime—the highest wages ever received in seafarers' history. The American Steamship Owners' Association and Admiral William S. Benson of the Shipping Board pointed out that the shipping business had slackened because of the worldwide economic depression of 1920–21, that thousands of seamen in Atlantic ports were standing in soup lines, and that some 30,000 seamen were out of work. They proposed some changes: Replacement of three watches with two (that is, a compulsory 12-hour day instead of eight, or 84 hours a week instead of 56), coupled with a 15 per cent wage cut and elimination of all overtime. In addition, they insisted on a nonunion open shop and the removal of union officials' right to visit ships.

It was enough to bring out Furuseth's militancy, full strength. He sought arbitration. His offer was rejected. Admiral Benson announced that on May 1, 1921, the new wages and conditions would go into effect on all government vessels—and the government now owned or leased 70 per cent of the American merchant marine. Any seaman who refused to work under the new rules would be out of work, would be locked out.

Senator La Follette called for a congressional investigation of the Shipping Boards' lockout, but he was unsuccessful. Furuseth asked that negotiations be continued, but Benson refused.

So the ISU called for a maritime strike. The Masters, Mates, and Pilots joined in sympathy. They managed to tie up most of the ships on both coasts for a short while, but the strike weakened quickly. Furuseth's attempt to reinstate the old "Oracle" tactic failed. The Pacific Coast longshoremen (with whom Furuseth was still feuding) refused to join in the strike, despite the fact that the sailors had from time to time supported the longshoremen when they needed help. The shipowners hired strikebreakers, some of whom were armed. Strikers were stabbed, scabs were beaten. Violence had returned to the waterfront. The shipowners asked for Federal troops and proposed that vessels be manned by naval reserves. They saw to it that the newspapers gave the strikers a bad press. They obtained injunctions against picketing.

A former police captain, Walter Peterson, spokesman for the Pacific Coast shipowners, told an investigator many years later, "I was hired during 1921 to break Andy Furuseth's union, and I broke it."

The membership of the ISU crumbled from 115,000 to 16,000 by 1923. In the SUP, it dropped from 8,781 to 1,300. Only the hard-core members remained. To them, Furuseth wrote, "The battle is fought and lost. We have lost many battles before . . . To the real fighter for ideals a battle lost means nothing. Let us accept the real situation as men, who have higher thoughts than a few cents more wages and a few minutes less work per day. He that would earn money shall lose it; but he that is willing to lose money for principles' sake shall gain it—after awhile. Not now."

Furuseth must surely have been despondent. And if he had known that "after awhile" would not come for 13 years, until 1934, he would have been even more so.

Part of his despondency was caused by the caliber of men in the union. There remained only a few "real" sailors, those who knew how to man a sailing ship. In the days before, no sailor could join the SUP until he had passed an examination. It was held before two elder able seamen in a room with all sorts of ropes and gear. The candidate was asked many questions, such as, "Where will the hauling part of the fore topsail halyard on board a four-mast bark be standing?" Most of these new fellows didn't know the answer.

The fact that they were going to work on a steamship, and not a sailing vessel, didn't impress Furuseth. Seamanship was a craft, and no man was a "real" sailor unless he was a master of the craft.

Furuseth felt that there was something else lacking in the new steamship sailors. When he tried to get them to use the "Oracle" technique during the strike, they were unwilling to sacrifice their jobs or part of their pay for the benefit of the union. Furuseth recalled the sacrifices willingly made by others in the past, and it was often difficult to conceal his contempt for those unwilling to give up a day's pay to help the cause. He pleaded with them, but they ignored his pleas, often shouting back in defiance.

Now, with all his other losses, Furuseth was also losing his men, the sailors to whom he had dedicated his life. They accepted the benefits of his labor over more than a quarter century, but they blamed their present sorry condition on what they declared was his misguided devotion to an outmoded craft unionism. He was, they said, old-fashioned, unable to change with the times.

They were listening to the cry for "One Big Union." They were listening to and following a group that Furuseth detested . . . the Wobblies.

Chapter Eight

Furuseth was now approaching 70 years of age. As he grew older, he became thinner; and as he grew thinner, he appeared taller, although somewhat stoop-shouldered. His hair had become completely white, and his strong hook-nose and deep wrinkles gave his face a harsh expression. Someone said that the profile of his Norse face stood out "like the prow of a Viking ship," while others said he looked more like an Indian chief than a Norwegian sailor. One old-timer said, "He always reminded me of an eagle, with his beak. He looked stern. And he was a guy always on the go. Even when he got old, he looked like a guy who really wanted to get around. Sure was busy."

And he had a reason to be busy. Another gang was threatening his sailors.

Furuseth's International Seamen's Union was a federation of craft unions, composed entirely of seamen. Samuel Gompers and the AFL believed that the entire labor union movement should be limited to skilled workmen, tightly organized into craft unions. The Industrial Workers of the World (IWW), or the "Wobblies" as they were popularly known, had been founded in 1905 in Chicago in response to the AFL's craft union policy—opposition to unionism for unskilled workers. They proposed to expropriate the means of production and to put the working class in "possession of the world." They advocated the use of sabotage and the general strike to advance the cause of labor.

The Wobblies formed "industrial unions" to include all workers within each particular industry—such as mining, agriculture, maritime, and such—rather than by specific crafts. They believed in and preached "One Big Union." For the maritime industry, they organized the Marine Transport Workers Industrial Union, and sought members from among the seamen, longshoremen, warehousemen, teamsters, and any other trade that had any connection with the maritime industry.

Furuseth believed in autonomous craft unions, and strongly opposed uniting the seamen's welfare with shore workers—especially with longshoremen. He declared, "How landsmen, who know nothing about seamen's lives and seamen's traditions and do not care to know, can possibly 'safeguard' the economic interests of the seamen will always remain a mystery to me."

The conflict between craft unionism and "syndicalist unionism" (as it was called) became as bitter as the struggle between workers and employers. Fususeth vowed to fight the Wobblies to the end. And he did.

But many of the sailors leaned toward the IWW. The Wobblies spoke for some of the most exploited and oppressed groups of workers in the United States. The sailors were keenly aware of the distance between the lives of the rich and poor. They were open to revolutionary ideas.

One of the old-timers who sided with Furuseth said, "The Wobblies—the sons-of-bitches—called themselves the Transport Workers Union, and they said, 'Are you for peace?' We said, 'Of course.' Well then they got us to sign up."

Then he talked about the Centralia Massacre. In the state of Washington, working conditions and wages were deplorable for the "bindle stiffs" (itinerant loggers who carried their blanket rolls from job to job). The Wobblies moved in, urging the loggers and sawmill workers to organize, and preaching "One Big Union" and overthrow of the capitalistic system. They were considered a threat by local businessmen and Legionnaires in Centralia.

During a parade on Armistice Day, hell suddenly broke loose. A shower of bullets flew in all directions. Legionnaires attacked and ransacked the Wobbly Hall. Several men fell, some wounded and some dead. A man name Everest, who had shot and killed a Legionnaire, was put in jail and then at night dragged out to be lynched and mauled.

Dozens of Wobblies were arrested. At a subsequent trial, the prosecution sought to prove that unarmed marching men were fired on by the IWW in a murder conspiracy; the defense sought to show they were merely trying to defend against an attack on the Wobbly Hall. Eight Wobblies were sentenced to prison for 25 to 40 years.

Although the public in general opposed the IWW, there were those who supported the Wobblies in their struggle to protect the "downtrodden and oppressed." Many sailors felt a sense of working class brotherhood with their fellow workers in the sawmills and logging camps in the Northwest.

The Furuseth supporter summed up: "And so a hell of a lot of the guys left the Sailors' Union and joined the Wobblies. All they had to do was make martyrs of some kind."

The Wobblies created a sense of camaraderie. At the end of each meeting, and sometimes in waterfront saloons, they sang songs:

> *Work and pray, live on hay*
> *For you'll get pie in the sky when you die*

And another:

Hold the fort for we are coming—
Union men be strong.
Side by side we battle onward,
Victory will come.

Fierce and long the battle rages,
But we will not fear,
Help will come when e'er it's needed,
Cheer, my Comrades, cheer.

The Wobblies sought to advance the cause of labor in what they saw as primarily an economic struggle. But eventually the IWW came under the control of anarchists and syndicalists who were more interested in wielding political power and disrupting the social order. Unions could be used as a basis for immediate social revolution. That fact, together with the IWW's strong opposition to World War I, led to the suppression of its press and to prosecutions under the Espionage and Sedition Acts of 1917 and 1918. After the war, many states adopted legislation outlawing the IWW and making it a crime to produce, possess, or circulate printed matter supporting "criminal syndicalism." Many of the Wobbly leaders were sent to jail.

Despite these obstacles, the Marine Transport Workers Union—a creation of the Wobbly movement—continued to thrive. As it gained in strength, the SUP and the ISU became weaker and weaker.

Furuseth viewed the rise of the Wobblies with alarm and anger. He opposed everything they stood for. And now they were filling his sailors with "radical" ideas, were stealing them away from his union. Well, he would see about that.

One of the Wobblies' victories was the election of J.

Vance Thompson as the new editor of the *Coast Seamen's Journal*. He replaced Paul Scharrenberg, who was both an associate and close friend of Furuseth's. Although not a member of the IWW, Thompson sympathized with its ideas and used the *Journal* to foster them. To Furuseth's disgust, he advocated a closer alliance between the seamen and the shore workers, including the longshoremen.

In 1921, the IWW was promoting a strike which Furuseth believed should be settled. Thompson used the *Journal* to encourage the rejection of a proposed settlement agreement. The members of the SUP voted almost unanimously to reject the contract. From his Washington office, Furuseth blasted the "incomprehensible stupidity" of the West Coast seamen, and lamented that the "work of years and years is going into the waste-basket." He rushed back to San Francisco and called a mass meeting at the Civic Auditorium. Completely fired up, he invoked the spirit of all the past martyrs of the union, castigated his opponents, and challenged a demonstration of personal loyalty to himself. He aroused the members to such a high pitch that it is said Thompson and his supporters trembled for their lives. Police were called, and after a riotous meeting the membership voted two to one in favor of accepting the new contract—a complete reversal of the previous almost-unanimous decision. This was a demonstration of Furuseth's dynamic personality, even at this advanced age.

Next, he took steps to rid his union of the radical element. He addressed meetings of sailors, to whom he charged that the IWW had been secretly organized by the shipowners, and intimated that the owners would like to see the sailors join with the Wobblies so that they could be put in jail under the criminal syndicalism laws. He charged the IWW with every misdeed he could think of. He laid down an ultimatum, stating that there was no room in the union for both himself and Thompson. The union members refused to repudiate the old Viking warrior, the legendary figure who had done so much for the seafaring men. Thompson was ousted as editor and expelled from the union along with 30 of his closest sympathizers.

Despite this setback, the Transport Workers Union continued to grow. It gained membership, called many "quickie strikes," and culminated its activities with a general strike in 1923. But at that high water mark, the IWW began to feel the mounting pressure from its enemies. The police broke up its meetings, arrested the leaders for violation of the criminal syndicalism laws, and made them subject to prison sentences of from one to 14 years. Mass arrests were made, and a steady stream of Wobblies was herded to San Quentin prison. Vigilantes from the Ku Klux Klan and the American Legion conducted a series of raids on the IWW halls. Some organizers were kidnapped and tarred and feathered. This concentrated opposition was too much to overcome. With many of its leaders in jail, the influence of the IWW dwindled away.

The formal organization of the IWW ultimately collapsed, but the spirit behind it lingered on among the seamen. They were weary of exploitation and impatient with talk. The philosophy of the Wobblies continued to have strong appeal.

Furuseth refused to see that the sentiment of the rank and file was increasingly swinging over to the radicals. The members of the SUP still respected Furuseth for his past efforts, but they began to resent his dictatorial methods. At one meeting, when he gave a speech condemning the "reds and radicals," he was met by heckling and jeers. When he insisted on adjourning the meeting immediately after his speech, the members jumped up and shouted their protests. The police were called to protect Furuseth from the angry members. But he ignored the protests, and continued to insist that sailors should be organized in independent craft unions. He declared that their goals could best be achieved through legislation and the courts.

So, back to Washington went the stubborn head of the union. He spent the rest of his life lobbying to enforce the Seamen's Act. But the union's defeat in the 1921 strike had so strengthened the shipowners that it marked the end of any help to the unions from Congress until the New Deal legislation under President Roosevelt. Bills introduced through Furuseth's efforts usually dragged slowly through Congress for years, and then were dropped. He failed to secure the passage of a single important piece of new legislation. However, it was not all in vain. Bills introduced by the shipowners to weaken the Act by reducing A.B. requirements and lowering safety provisions were vigorously fought by Furuseth, and were eventually defeated.

He again turned to the courts rather than Congress for relief, still personally deciding what cases to try and how they should be tried.

From 1920 to 1935, Furuseth went to Europe seven times on behalf of the International Seamen's Union. He strove to extend the principles of the Seamen's Act to European nations and to protect the interests of seamen. One year, he stayed in Europe for six months, visiting different ports to determine the methods by which aliens were being smuggled into the United States under the guise of seamen. He consistently opposed all international treaties, fearing that the United States would have to adopt lower standards set by such a treaty, replacing the standards in the Seamen's Act.

But his views were contrary to those of other leaders in the labor movement. The delegates to each meeting he attended were not eager to hear Furuseth repeat once again his appeal to free the seamen, but out of respect they usually consented to hear him out. He expressed his opinions with vigor, but in voting was always in the minority—sometimes, the minority of one.

Furuseth's stubborn refusal to modify his conservative ideas to conform to the changing views of the members began to alienate him from other leaders in the labor movement. And it is one of the great ironies in his life that, although he was a steadfast conservative, the person who was perhaps his best friend, Senator Robert La Follette, was an uncompromising liberal.

Furuseth continued to have Sunday breakfast in the La Follette home, and at other times visited until late hours of the night. Andy and Bob had become intimate friends. Although they had been born only one year apart, they started life much differently. La Follette was born in a log cabin in Wisconsin, of French Huguenot and Scotch-Irish heritage. Both his great-grandfathers fought in the American Revolutionary War. Furuseth, of pure Norwegian stock, first saw the light of day in an isolated part of an isolated country. They each had a different social status. One was a congressman, governor, senator, and eventually a candidate for the presidency of the United States. The other was a man from before the mast and a union officer.

And yet, something had drawn these two men together to produce a great piece of legislation: the La Follette Seamen's Act of 1915. Each gave credit for the Act to the other, but, in truth, it needed both. It needed the inspiration and enduring enthusiasm of Furuseth, and the parliamentary skill of La

Follette. La Follette considered the Act one of his most worthwhile accomplishments; to Furuseth, it constituted his life's work.

When La Follette had led the opposition to the U.S. entry into World War I, Furuseth had joined with him and had been outspoken in all aspects of the opposition. Silas Axtell, Furuseth's legal advisor, wrote to Furuseth, warning him to back off. "(P)ublic opinion is highly inflamed on the subject of Pacifism and Pro-Germanism . . . If the Seamen's Union should go on record for pacifism or openly for Senator La Follette, they would in the average mind be forming the conclusion that seafarers were disloyal. We all know that this is not so, and you and I know what effect that would have on our higher courts. The interpretation of laws in the past have partaken of the spirit of the age in which they were enacted and interpreted. It will be so now . . . We have every reason to expect that the Supreme Court of the United States will place upon this statute (the Seamen's Act) the interpretation which we believe is the correct one. For Heaven's sake, don't do anything which will jeopardize our chances."

Furuseth ignored the warning and continued to openly support La Follette in his opposition to the war.

Despite Furuseth's conviction that the unions should stay out of politics, that didn't prevent him from helping his friend Bob in his political career. In 1916, he went to Wisconsin to support La Follette in a primary race. When questioned why he had temporarily deserted his union duties in Washington, Furuseth explained that La Follette's enemies were crucifying him for his support of the Seamen's Act. When he later acknowledged to himself that the "people of Wisconsin know practically nothing about the Seamen's Act and they care less," this didn't stop him from returning to Wisconsin in the fall. He went again to lobby and to raise campaign funds in 1920 and 1922. In 1924, La Follette was nominated as the Progressive-Labor Party candidate for president of the United States. Furuseth travelled about and enthusiastically campaigned for him. (Although defeated, La Follette made a good showing.)

La Follette initiated and supported legislation that Furuseth sought. These two men helped each other and had much in common. Their parallels are striking:

Both were inspiring speakers and competent writers, and both used their talents effectively to promote what they believed in.

Both were leaders in the struggle of "common people" against the special interests. "Fighting Bob" La Follette fought primarily for the farmers against the railroad corporations and banks. (Furuseth fought for the sailors against the shipowners.)

La Follette founded and published the *La Follette's Magazine* to expound on his views. (Furuseth had the *Coast Seamen's Journal.*)

La Follette was an honest man who had the courage to fight corruption wherever he saw it. Believing that the war had given large corporations nearly complete control over the federal government, he set out to expose the most flagrant corruption of the postwar years. Among others, he initiated the investigation of Teapot Dome and other naval oil leases that led to the exposure of fraud and conspiracy in the Harding Administration. It took courage to oppose the establishment.

La Follette was often maligned by those who opposed him. As mentioned, after the filibuster against the Armed Ship Bill and his vote against the entry of the United States into World War I, he was denounced and burned in effigy. Some senators and many prominent men and women demanded his expulsion from the Senate. At various times, he was called a "traitor," a "high priest of radicalism," and similar degrading epithets. (Furuseth was called an "armchair sailor," a "grafter," an "informer," and a "tool of the shipowners.")

Both were independent thinkers. Although elected as a Republican, La Follette often ignored the dictates of the party leaders. He supported President Wilson, a Democrat, on domestic policies, and occasionally was the only Republican to vote against the party line. (At times, Furuseth took the side of the shipowners and against the union if he thought the owners were in the right.)

Probably as a result of this independence, at a Republican caucus in Washington, a resolution was adopted that La Follette not be invited to future Republican conferences, and not be named to fill any Republican vacancies in the Senate. (Furuseth had a similar rebuff. At an important International Conference for Safety of Life at Sea held in London, the Department of Commerce asked William Green, then president of the AFL, to name a labor representative to be a member of the American delegation. Furuseth was the logical person to fill the position, but Green was familiar with Furuseth's attitude toward international treaties, and chose not to select him. Since it would not have been diplomatic to invite any other member of the ISU, no one was named. Furuseth understood the situation, and was deeply hurt.)

Both Furuseth and La Follette had resilience. The day after La Follette's defeat in the presidential election, he was not depressed or embittered by the result, but "looked upon it as merely another skirmish lost." He began making plans at once to organize the progressive votes for the next campaign. ("Tomorrow is also a day.")

So, despite the differences in background and social

status of La Follette and Furuseth, there was a common bond, a series of parallels, that drew them and held them together as close friends.

However, there was one big difference in the lives of these two men. La Follette died in 1925, but Furuseth was fated to live another 13 years—bitter years in which he had to fight yet another organized group, and then had to face a condition, a force, so powerful that it ultimately destroyed him. And he had to fight these battles without the help and companionship of his friend Bob La Follette. He had to fight the last battles alone.

Chapter Nine

The American Communist movement started in 1919, just two years after the Russian Revolution. Its first manifesto proclaimed that capitalism was in collapse and that America was ripe for revolution. The rank-and-file members, never large in numbers, had only a hazy grasp of Moscow's current thoughts and goals. Many joined the Party full of enthusiasm and then, disillusioned, dropped out after a short time. But one of Lenin's most important organizational principles was that a revolution required a corps of professionals, a well-trained and dedicated cadre that would follow orders explicitly, and that would, without question or hesitation, shift directions whenever ordered to do so. This is what gave the Party an influence all out of proportion to its size.

Moscow formed the Red International of Labor Unions, but Furuseth ignored it, the Wobblies rejected affiliation, and it had no effect on the American maritime unions.

Then Joseph Stalin came to power in 1924. As would prove typical of his subsequent actions, he constantly changed goals and tactics. At first, he ordered that the American trade unions be destroyed by "boring from within." Then he switched, directing the members to form new unions to compete with the existing ones. The names of communist organizations were constantly changed. The members jumped every time the Party (that is, Stalin) spoke, never knowing why changes were being made, but always following orders from Moscow.

On April 26, 1930, about 180 delegates from port cities around the nation gathered in New York City to form yet another union: the Marine Workers Industrial Union. This was an industrial organization of seamen, longshoremen, and other harbor workers. More that half of the delegates had once been Wobblies. It was claimed that only a handful of Communists were in the delegation, but it is evident that they played a leading role. The union's preamble declared that, "The MWIU urges upon all its members the most active participation in the general struggles of the working class, economic and political, directed toward the goal of establishment of a revolutionary workers' government." The convention also resolved that they "will defend the Soviet Union, the only workers' government in the world."

The Communist Party stood for everything that Furuseth detested. It was a radical and collectivist organization; loyal to the Soviet Union rather than to America; stressing political rather than economic goals; a proponent of industrial, rather than craft, unionism; and an organization that engaged in lies, slander, violence, and disruption. It recklessly vilified the other maritime unions, calling the ISU "labor fakers," the longshoremen's union "corrupt," and the Wobblies "a few degenerate, spittoon philosophers."

Furuseth had had experience before with the Communist Party. Back in 1924, when Bob La Follette ran for president, the Communists had tried to take control of the Progressive-Labor Party. But La Follette repudiated them. The Communists responded with biting attacks on La Follette. Furuseth had vivid memories of their tactics, and fought them whenever he could. Now, the Communists viciously and relentlessly attacked Furuseth with a campaign of character assassination. He was an obstacle to be removed.

The old man already had enough problems with the

shipowners without having the Communists assailing him. Ever since the disastrous strike of 1921, the Waterfront Employers' Union of San Francisco, with their fink hiring halls, had complete dominance in maritime labor relations. Furuseth continued to try to inspire his men with brave talk, but he couldn't overcome the power of the shipowners. Wages had been lowered, hours had been lengthened, and working conditions had been worsened. In the intervening years, unionism on the waterfront hit an all-time low in numbers, finances, and morale.

Moreover, Furuseth still had to contend with the Wobblies. He claimed that the shipowners gave employment to members of the IWW while refusing employment to his own union men. The shipowners' purpose was to use the Wobblies to divide and disrupt his union, then they could take care of the Wobblies through the syndicalism laws. Their scheme was working, because the membership in the IWW increased while that in Furuseth's ISU and SUP declined.

His conflict with the longshoremen had become even more intense. The two unions had always had their jurisdictional fights: Who should load and unload the ships? It was an ancient conflict, periodically flaring up. Now the longshoremen were returning to an earlier policy of raiding work away from the sailors. Over the years, the sailors had at times supported the longshoremen in their labor disputes. Sometimes the longshoremen made gains; the sailors, seldom, if ever. "The sailors," Furuseth said "have been mercilessly and pitilessly used by the longshoremen." He would no longer listen to the old tune, "Play Up The Band, Here Comes The Sailor." He was no longer willing to let his men be used by others. He had to fight to retain his craft union. He had to resist industrial unionism.

And now he had to fight the Communists.

Furuseth might have been able to continue standing up to all his adversaries, might have been able to overcome all the obstacles. But a condition arose that would destroy him. An irresistible force to which he could not adjust, one to which he was unwilling or unable to yield. Something called Changing Times.

The Great Depression brought economic stagnation and mass unemployment. As the Depression deepened, American public opinion gradually drifted away from support of individualism, and swung over towards support of collectivism and more active government involvement in economic affairs. The public began to demand that the "government *do* something." And down on the waterfront, tens of thousands of workers were unemployed and hungry; they were swept along with this shift in tides.

Furuseth's character had been developed during the old sailing ship days "when ships were made of wood and men were made of iron." He regarded his American citizenship very seriously, and could quote verbatim the Declaration of Independence, which he described as "that fundamental Christian ideal or law that men are created equal and by their Creator endowed with certain inalienable rights, among which is the right to life, to liberty, and to the pursuit of happiness. But," Furuseth stressed, "the pursuit, if you please. No human being or institution can give or guarantee happiness; but we can have an equal right to pursue it."

The reason he objected to industrial unionism was that he believed that "Crafts are essential to civilization . . . Skill is the development of the ages, and civilization goes onward and onward as men develop skill, and civilization dies as men forget how to develop it."

In his address to the students of the University of

California in Berkeley on Labor Day in 1927, he said, "Work is worship—to labor is to pray, because that is to exercise the highest, the divine faculties implanted in us as the sons of God. It matters not if the labor be the writing of a thesis or the digging of a ditch, it is the use of the same divine faculty to labor—to create—and upon its proper and free use depends the life of individuals, nations, and races."

He claimed that the "radicals" viewed work as a duty to be endured, and preferably avoided. "Although these men always pretend to seek employment, they are never seen at work." Furuseth was certain that they would help destroy the skill of the craftsman.

Nor could he adjust to the loosening of business morals. Once he was invited to accept a free cruise through the Panama Canal to the New Orleans ISU convention on the United Fruit Company's ship. He figured United Fruit wasn't giving a free cruise to him for nothing. He explained, "In all my life I have been looking for the person who really wanted to give something to a seaman for nothing, and I have not found that creature in the jungle anywhere." He turned down the offer—more evidence of his unwillingness to conform to accepted ways of doing business.

Some of his fixed ideas appear harsh and unfeeling:

He opposed workmen's compensation, but did so because he felt it relieved the shipowner of responsibility, and made negligence by insurance profitable to the owners by putting the burden of maintaining the cripples, widows, and orphans on the public after the pittance of compensation was exhausted.

He opposed liability insurance, but only because it would minimize and practically wipe away the shipowner's liability to maintain a safe ship. Sometimes a vessel was so heavily insured as to be worth more at the bottom of the sea than afloat.

He even opposed the union-controlled hiring hall, because he regarded it as an unworkable nuisance and a violation of a seaman's right to seek employment without interference by any middleman. And also because the captain of a ship had the responsibility for its safety, and should therefore have the freedom to select his own crew.

Furuseth was a rugged individualist, a Jeffersonian Democrat, who opposed government interference in the lives of men. "We must depend upon our own strength or die." Furuseth distrusted the government, and distrusted any advantage claimed for a policy that didn't rely solely on the stamina and courage and wisdom of the seamen themselves.

Maybe today, upon reflection, we might concede that there is some merit to parts of his philosophy. But it is certain that he was utterly out of step with the general thinking of the '30s. He failed to understand that what he called "amalgamation"—industrial unionism—was becoming more and more attractive to the workers. Many members regarded the separation of crafts in the maritime industry as highly artificial. Even the other leaders in his own unions disagreed with his views. He was that proverbial lonely voice crying in the wilderness—and he would suffer the consequences of his inflexibility.

He did not understand that he would lose what he valued the most. He would lose the support of his own men. The sailors would turn against him.

The beginning of the end of Andrew Furuseth's career occurred with the coming of the San Francisco Maritime Strike of 1934.

Chapter Ten

One of the first actions of Franklin D. Roosevelt as president was passage of the National Industrial Recovery Act, which recognized and protected unions as employee representatives. About the same time, unions were powerfully aided by an anti-injunction law. Furuseth had sought it for years. This law made it easier for workers to go on strike. As a result, in 1933 a national strike wave swept across the country, involving the automobile and soft coal industries, the United Mine Workers, the Ladies' Garment Workers, and many others.

The San Francisco waterfront now had 82 docks capable of handling 250 ships at a time. Trucks rumbled across the broad, cobblestoned Embarcadero. Locomotives hissed and clanged as they dragged freight cars along the tracks of the State-owned Belt Line Railroad. Across the Embarcadero from the docks, one could still see seamen's outfitting companies, cafeterias, saloons, pool halls, and cheap hotels. Giant skyscrapers loomed up in the background.

The haunting wail of the Alcatraz foghorns would warn that fog was swooping in through the Golden Gate. But even when the foghorns were silent, a gray pallor hung over the waterfront. The Depression bore down heavily.

The average wages for an able seaman was 36 dollars a month . . . when he could get work.

A longshoreman could make 85 cents an hour, which was pretty good . . . if he could find a job. To obtain work, a longshoreman had to get up before dawn to take his chances in the "shape," where the day's hirings were selected from among an anxious crowd. Not picked, he could hang around the waterfront, or trudge from wharf to wharf, but the likelihood of his landing a job was almost nonexistent. What was necessary was to kowtow to the straw bosses who did the hiring. Jobs usually went to the cap-in-hand type who understood the wisdom of handing over a kickback or buying a few drinks. Maybe after three or four days, or maybe a week, he might get a job, which might last a day, two days, or maybe just a few hours. Then he had to start looking again.

When he did get a job it had to be as a member of the Longshoremen's Association of San Francisco, a company union. If he took any interest in trying to join another union, he was blacklisted and unable to find work on any dock.

In the latter part of 1932, a small mimeographed publication, the *Waterfront Worker*, began to appear on the docks and in places where longshoremen herded together. It is still uncertain who actually published it. It called for the destruction of the company Blue Book and for the formation of a rank-and-file union. Although the little paper was clumsily put together, it expressed in plain and frank language the resentment that had been gnawing at the waterfront workers for years.

With the passage of the National Recovery Act, and partly as a result of the agitational work of the *Waterfront Worker*, a new union was formed in San Francisco. It was a local of the International Longshoremen's Association, an affiliate of the AFL.

Uptown, in a converted store across from the Civic Center, the Communist Party had its local headquarters and a book store. It openly published its own newspaper. It conducted schools, open forums, and meetings, as well as demonstrations and parades. It had tried to organize the workers in the Marine Workers Industrial Union, with minimum success, and had viciously attacked the AFL unions. But now it received orders from higher up to cease the condemnations and instead to infiltrate those unions, including the new ILA. It did so with vigor, pretending as if its previous attacks had never occurred. A handful of Communists began to hang around the wharves, mingling with the longshoremen, and sometimes mounting soapboxes. Communists became members of the International Longshoremen's Association.

Now that the workers had the right to join unions of their own choosing and to bargain collectively, longshoremen flocked into the ILA. They abandoned the Blue Book and dropped out of the company union.

The employers refused to recognize the ILA.

So, the battle was joined.

The ILA union made certain demands, which the employers flatly turned down. The longshoremen elected a rank-and-file committee, and took a strike vote. The federal government started mediation, but neither side would budge.

On May 9, after a month of tension along the waterfront, the longshoremen went on strike in San Francisco, Seattle, Tacoma, Portland, San Pedro, San Diego, Stockton, Bellingham—all the Pacific Coast ports.

In San Francisco, about 1,000 angry pickets gathered around the 60 ships in port. On May 13, the teamsters went out. Two days later, they were joined by the three independent unions which were members of the International Seamen's Union (the sailors, the stewards, and the unlicensed engine room workers). Soon, all the maritime unions were on strike. They had their own reasons—"low wages and rotten conditions prevailing"—but the longshoremen provided the trigger.

The shipowners brought in strikebreakers, who ambushed and beat the strikers with fists and clubs. Union gangs, in turn, waylaid the scabs and roughed them up. The violence intensified, then erupted. Ambulances sped along the waterfront, police sirens screamed.

Furuseth, in Washington at the time, was taken by surprise. He wrote to George Larsen, a local union official, asking for information. He wondered if the strike was under the control of the unions, or was it "really under the management of the Communists?"

Larsen replied by telegraph: "The Communists are loudmouthed but not in control," and he explained the details of the situation.

Furuseth answered, "I am glad of the action you have taken. I could not see any other thing to be done . . . (T)his should bring back to the Union a lot of feeling that once belonged to it."

Furuseth welcomed the strike because he could foresee that it might bring about a rejuvenation of the SUP and the ISU. What he could not foresee was that the strike would widen the gap between his conservatism and the growing militancy of the rank and file—that his unions might forge ahead, but leave him behind. He could not foresee the lurking danger in the impending changes.

Long picket lines paraded up and down in front of the docks, in violation of an anti-picketing ordinance that had long been ignored. One day, at Pier 18, the police, on foot and on horse, tried to drive the pickets away. They swung their clubs. The strikers retaliated with fists and bricks. More police appeared and released a barrage of tear gas. The strikers retreated to the longshoremen's headquarters . . . in the Audiffred Building, the former location of the SUP.

Other confrontations took place. The *Chronicle* reported, "Two hundred and fifty Communists and police staged a bloody battle yesterday afternoon near the Embarcadero—the second major riot to mark the longshoremen's strike this week. Nineteen persons were treated at hospitals as a result, and two youths were reported to have been shot and subsequently spirited away in the ensuing confusion. Scores of others were injured."

Joseph P. Ryan, international president of the ILA, came to San Francisco. A conservative labor leader, he was opposed to the strike and concerned that it was being manipulated by the Communists. He met with the employers and worked out an agreement with them. He signed the agreement, claiming it was satisfactory to the union members, although they knew nothing of its contents. When he appeared before an ILA membership meeting and waved the agreement in the air, a dock worker, who spoke with what sounded like a cockney accent, stood up, verbally analyzed the agreement and blasted it as a trick. The members booed Ryan and voted against the agreement. The agitator, Harry Bridges, was cheered, and he started his career as one of the best known labor leaders in America.

Born in Australia, Bridges went to sea, got off a sailing ship in San Francisco in 1920, and joined Furuseth's Sailors' Union of the Pacific. He participated in the 1921 seamen's strike as a picket captain in New Orleans. Disgusted with the conservative policies of the Furuseth leadership, he joined the IWW, but soon dropped out of that. In 1922, he left the sea and began working as a longshoreman on the San Francisco docks.

He hated the company union (the Blue Book), was in constant trouble with the stevedoring employers, and opposed them whenever he could. Although he was convinced that "the class struggle is here," he refused to join the Marine Workers Industrial Union. He admitted subsequently that he used the Communist Party and its members to help him in his labor battles, but denied that he was ever a member of the Party—and despite several court trials in later years, the government could not prove that he was. Now he headed an "independent" group of ILA dock workers, and, after the encounter with Ryan, was ready to lead the strike.

How much control the Communist Party had in the strike is not known for sure. Undoubtedly, some of the professionals took influential positions in the AFL unions, and played active roles. Its newspapers and propaganda apparatus were used effectively to promote its goals. Its skillful and disciplined organizational ability was evident in some of the actions. And it lured in many new members from among the frustrated seamen and longshoremen and the disenchanted Wobblies. But the new recruits didn't stay in for long. As one ex-Communist said, he fought hard from within the Party for better working conditions, racial equality, and free speech, but left "because the Commies don't really want these reforms. They want to use the lack of them to win their own game."

So, the real Communists were relatively few in number, and their influence has probably been exaggerated.

For one thing, the newspapers were so anti-labor that they attributed all strike activity to the Communists. Time after time, their headlines and text referred not to the "strikers" but to the "Communists," as though all of the strikers were Communists. Business leaders and politicians declared that the Communists had captured the unions so they could paralyze the city, and that their avowed purpose was to provoke class hatred and bloodshed and to take over the United States government. They wanted revolution. There were even rumors—carried in the newspapers—that a Red Army was approaching San Francisco. Whether this wave of hysteria was planted by the employers or not, it resulted in turning public sentiment against the strikers.

The Communists eagerly accepted the "blame," and even invented additional reports of their successes. With newspapers, leaflets, and speech, they did all they could to foster the impression that they were more important than they really were.

So, how much control they had over the strike has never been certain. What is certain is that they carried on an unrelenting crusade to crucify Furuseth.

As part of its campaign, the Party vilified the conservative labor leaders of the AFL. Little effort was needed to attack Scharrenberg, Olander, and the other leaders, because most of the new breed of seamen had already turned against them. But Furuseth was a problem. The sailors usually exempted him from their criticism because of his earlier contributions to the seamen's welfare. They respected the "Old Man," the legendary figure who had freed them from slavery—conveniently ignoring that he was as conservative as the others; maybe even more so.

In order to degrade Furuseth, the Party charged that he was "in league" with the "company unions, the fink halls, the Blue Book, and the rest of the trash." They called him "Andy Barnacle" and "Weeping Willow Andy Feroshus." It was the Communists who had called the ill-fated 1921 strike despite Furuseth's opposition. And yet they now claimed that he sold out the union in that strike and would sell out the workers again.

The smear campaign was successful because the intemperate language against the venerable union leader was repeated often to new men who really knew little of union history and who scarcely knew the "Old Man of the Sea."

Up to this time, the maritime unions' main opposition was the Waterfront Employers' Union, represented by Thomas G. "Tear Gas" Plant. But with the rejection of Ryan's "settlement," the employers decided to bring in the big guns: The Industrial Association of San Francisco. This organization had about 1,000 members, including such giants as Southern Pacific Railroad, Standard Oil of California, Pacific Gas and Electric, Crocker National Bank, and others. So, the unions were no longer pitted against the shipowners alone, but were now faced with the power and influence of the area's entire business community.

The Industrial Association hired hundreds of strike-breakers and declared its intention to "open the port."

The unions countered by holding a public mass meeting in the Civic Auditorium. The hall was packed with thousands of men, chanting "We'll hang scabby Ryan from a sour apple tree." Harry Bridges, chairman of the Joint Strike Committee, was greeted with a wild ovation. When Mayor Rossi appeared, he was greeted by whistles and the stamping of feet. The boos and hissing became so thunderous that the mayor immediately escaped from the meeting, surrounded by blue uniforms. As members of the Strike Committee took the floor to explain their cause, the reaction of the men reached such a feverish pitch that now there was talk not only of a maritime strike, but of a general strike.

It was at this moment that 80-year-old Andy Furuseth

arrived in San Francisco from Washington by plane. He said that the strike could be settled within 24 hours. "The only thing which is standing in the way of settlement now is the mutual distrust of the employers for the men and the men for the employers. The first thing we must do is to re-establish this trust. We must make the employers and the men trust each other, and this strike will be settled and no harm done to anyone."

He was filled with high hopes for an early settlement.

He also declared, "We are keeping the Seamen's Union clean...We don't want any radicals or Communists or other trouble makers in our organization."

The day following his arrival, Furuseth appeared before the Longshoremen's Board, and enthusiastically started to outline a plan under which he proposed that everyone return to work pending arbitration.

The men on the Board wouldn't listen to him. "Look out for old Andy Barnacle. He'll sell us out again." The longshoremen turned thumbs down.

Furuseth was disappointed and angry. He knew he could never get along with the longshoremen, but they were even worse now that they were run by a bunch of Communist radicals. He was now convinced that they didn't want to settle the strike. They wanted to paralyze the shipping industry, wanted to shut down the city's business. Furuseth left the meeting in disgust.

The strikers had already picketed the wharves for eight weeks when the Industrial Association announced that the port would be opened on July 3. Police Chief William Quinn ordered the public away from the waterfront. The order produced the reverse of its intent. Now the sailors, longshoremen, and radicals were joined by hundreds of other persons who put on old clothes and came down to witness the excitement.

The Industrial Association decided to make its stand at Pier 38. In the early morning, nothing happened. About 11 a.m., police began moving in on foot, horseback, and in radio patrol cars. They cleared the pickets from outside Pier 38. Strikers, armed with bricks, cobblestones, railroad spikes, and clubs, waited impatiently. Nothing happened. At 1:27 p.m., the steel rolling doors lifted and five old trucks rolled out, proceeded by eight patrol cars. A police captain, standing on the running board of one of the patrol cars, raised a revolver in the air, and shouted, "The port is open."

All hell broke loose. Bricks, cobblestones, and other missiles flew through the air. Police on horseback (the "Horse Marines") swung their clubs, knocking strikers and onlookers to the ground. Some of the mounted police were dragged from their saddles and beaten to the pavement. Dozens of skirmishes broke out. Clouds of tear gas swept the picket lines and sent men choking in retreat. After four hours of fighting, 25 men, including nine policemen, were sent to the hospital. In order to avoid arrest, many of the bloodied strikers were taken to private homes to get patched up, and so weren't included in the statistics.

The next day was the Fourth of July. In honor of the day the Industrial Association announced trucking operations would cease, but would resume on July 5.

Furuseth wanted the sailors to return to work, provided the shipowners would agree to recognize the International Seamen's Union as their bargaining agent. All other matters, he thought, could be arbitrated. With his impassioned plea, he was able to persuade the members. They approved his proposal by a vote of 173 to 76 in a meeting held in the SUP San Francisco headquarters at 57 Clay Street.

But when he went to San Pedro to get an endorsement, the members there booed him! They turned down the plan. They wanted to stick with the longshoremen!

Furuseth was stunned. For years, he had to fight the longshoremen . . . as well as the shipowners, the crimps, the radicals, and the others. He had to stand up to them all. And why had he done it? He had done it for his own men, the sailors, so that they could have freedom, so they could have the rights that other people had. And now, for the first time, *his own men* had turned against him. Those with whom he had walked side by side, now turned their backs to him. They had booed him, had rejected him!

Furuseth struggled against depression. What human reaction can cause as much heartache as that of being rejected by those you care for? Furuseth felt deeply hurt, depressed. He tried to console himself with the thought that the San Pedro incident had been an anomaly, a minor setback that could be corrected. Surely, the men would come about. "Tomorrow is also a day."

On the morning of July 5, a special meeting of the Sailors' Union was called in San Francisco—this time stacked against Furuseth. The previous approval of his proposal was reversed by a vote of 459 to 95. The members refused to settle independently of the longshoremen. Furuseth argued that the sailors should go it alone, but they refused.

"Why have my men turned against me?" he cried out. For 40 years he had been taking care of his men, and they had followed his lead. And now the longshoremen were using the sailors to gain power for themselves. Couldn't they see that? Maybe, he thought, it might have been different if he had the vote of the real sailors, the old-timers he had worked with over the years. It wasn't the same with these new men, packed in a hall and incited by those who had their own selfish interests in mind. The sailor had always been the forgotten man, with no one to depend on but himself. He should stand alone, should fight for his own rights. And this time the differences could be settled by arbitration. The sailors should go back to work. There was no need to strike.

He pleaded with the men.

But they would not listen.

That very day, July 5, 1934, is still remembered as "Bloody Thursday."

The newspapers' reports that the Industrial Association would "open the port" at 8 a.m. on that day drew hundreds of pickets and other workingman sympathizers to the scene. It is said there were also thousands of spectators, some milling with the strikers and others watching from a safe distance.

At 7 a.m., a string of empty boxcars was sent rattling and banging down the Embarcadero behind a locomotive, forming a barricade. Nothing happened. Eyes were focused on the closed doors of Pier 38; faces were seen peering out from behind its dirty windows. An engine coughed inside the building.

At 8 a.m., the door slowly rose, and a truck ground its gears and shot out, the driver crouched low. A shout rang out from the pickets. Rocks and bricks bounced off the truck's fenders and hood. Without waiting, the police let loose with the tear gas. The battle began.

Widespread violence erupted instantaneously. A cop chased a striker and whacked him across the face with his nightstick. A half dozen longshoremen raced toward them, grabbed the policeman, and beat him to the ground. More cops ran over and began beating the longshoremen. Everywhere there was a waving of arms—swinging clubs, swinging fists, hurling bricks. Two boxcars burst into flames. Horses reared as mounted police dodged flying bricks. Unconscious pickets were dragged into ambulances or private cars and hauled away.

The Embarcadero and the streets nearby were crowded with people: longshoremen wearing their white caps, sailors, other workingmen who had come to join the action, high school and college kids, spectators, and even enterprising vendors peddling chocolate bars, chewing gum, and cigarettes. Office workers leaned out of windows.

The police tried to block the strikers from all directions. Every time the strikers made a move, the police fired tear gas and drove them back, clubs swinging. Gasping and choking, the mob retreated slowly to the base of Rincon Hill, then up its slope. The hill was swarming with people, and at its base stood about 20 cops, with their masks on, firing tear gas up at them. But the strikers had weapons of their own. Exposed outcroppings provided them with fragmented rocks, which they began flinging at the cops. The roar of the strikers' defiance crescendoed. Flying rocks showered the police. In response, they fired the first of the many revolver shots of the day. One, aimed high, whistled through the air and struck a window in a nearby house. Glass tinkled. The mob pulsated, and then, like molten lava, began to flow down the hill.

At the base, the police, reinforced by eight more carloads, were faced with a wall of angry men flooding toward them. Unable to stop them with tear gas, they fired their revolvers. The first victim was hit in the chest. He stumbled, but his momentum carried him to the base of the hill, where he collapsed on the sidewalk. Blood spurted from his body and dripped into the gutter.

Fierce hand-to-hand battles left the street littered with fallen bodies. The sound of sirens pierced the air. Ambulances and private cars raced to the scene.

By noon, a sudden quiet descended, as though a momentary truce had been declared while the bleeding bodies were collected and hauled away.

Most of the morning's fighting had taken place at the south end of the Embarcadero. Now, pickets drifted back to ILA headquarters in the Audiffred Building. They congregated outside, cursing and licking their wounds. Without warning, shortly after 1:00 p.m. the police swooped down in full force, staging a crushing surprise attack. From long range guns, the police fired shells through the ILA's windows, filling the headquarters with gas. The police moved in, firing pistols.

Outside the Audiffred Building, police gunfire shot and killed a longshoreman named Howard Sperry. Then they killed a Greek Communist cook named Nick Bordoise. These two deaths had wide repercussions. For one, it intensified the ferocity of the battle. The men went out with blood in their eyes. But no longer did they gather in large groups; instead they spread out in small, roving bands. "Then the gas won't do no good." The battlefield expanded to all that area south of Market Street, and a full seven blocks wide, running from the Embarcadero to Second Street. Struggling knots of strikers, closely pressed by the cops, scattered about. Many were in tattered clothes, sweaty, their hair matted with blood. Toughs from all over the city had come to the waterfront and joined in the melee. There were scores of riots, big and little; first here, now there.

Total confusion: . . . a cop on the ground, blood flowing from his head . . . the low boom of a gas gun . . . the howl of the sirens . . . clouds of tear gas darkening the sky . . . men vomiting in the streets . . . the crack of pistol fire . . . a man on his knees, struggling frantically to crawl away . . . the bellowings and curses of sweating men . . .

One newspaper reported, "Blood ran red in the streets of

San Francisco." Another: "Drip-drip-drip went the blood on the white tiled floor." And another: "A thin trickle of crimson crawls toward the curb."

The newspaper reporters had more than they could handle, running from one flare-up to another, often dodging bullets as they ran. Joe Rosenthal, a photographer for the *Daily News*, got shot in the ear, but he recovered and took many more photos. (Years later, during World War II, he took perhaps one of the most famous photographs of the century, the one showing marines raising a flag on Iwo Jima).

By the end of the day, the two men had been killed and 109 others lay badly injured in hospitals. A still larger number had been injured, but they had escaped or been carried away by friends, because being taken to a hospital meant automatic arrest.

The strikers named the day "Bloody Thursday," and even today workers on ships and docks stop work on July 5th in honor of the two men slain.

The funerals of Sperry and Bordoise brought about one of the most dramatic public demonstrations ever held in San Francisco. It was estimated that 25,000 people joined the funeral procession that marched up Market Street from the Ferry Building to the Civic Center. The parade was carried on with so much dignity and solemnity—heads bowed and bare; no one smoking, laughing, or speaking—that it played an important role in shifting public opinion over to the strikers . . . and helped to precipitate the next major move.

Two martyrs had been killed. What had been a rumble now became a roar. To *hell* with the maritime strike. Let's have a *general* strike. Tie up the *whole damn city!*

Chapter Eleven

The day after the funeral, 1,500 striking seamen met in the Sailors' Union of the Pacific hall. One of the local union officers tried to present a proposed settlement, but he was hooted down by the members. Furuseth eased the tension by rising to his feet to speak. His age was starting to show—his body appeared more frail, his voice weaker—and yet he spoke long and emotionally.

He told of incidents from early days of the union and of the obstacles they had to overcome. Eventually, he came to his main topic. He declared that the shipowners might be willing to arbitrate everything *except* the fink hall (the Marine Service Bureau, the company-controlled hiring hall). "If you were to tell me" he said, "that you (would accept the other terms) and were willing to go to work through the fink hall, and asked me to go to the shipowners with the proposition—I'd tell you to *go to hell.*"

The members rose to their feet with wild applause.

The next day, typewritten petitions were anonymously prepared and circulated. Among other things, they repudiated Furuseth as a seamen's representative to hearings to be held before the National Longshoremen's Board (the strike mediation board). But Furuseth still retained some standing, and went as a representative. He continually interrupted the proceedings.

"This hearing is getting nowhere," he said. "There is an

agreement between the banks and the Industrial Association and the shipowners. This board should get the truth about it, and the only way you can get the truth is to use the full powers granted this board by law, and subpoena their records, bylaws, and constitutions."

Later on, he addressed the board again. "Gentlemen, may I suggest that you are merely wasting your time here? You can't get the truth this way. Go to the bottom of this thing. Find out who is who. Use your powers."

As Furuseth predicted, the mediation board failed to accomplish anything. The Industrial Association continued to insist on the Shipping Board's hiring hall, but made half-hearted gestures at reconciliation on other matters. The strikers would have none of it.

A general strike had been discussed by agitators for more than a month as the way to settle the waterfront deadlock. The killing of Sperry and Bordoise provided the spark that set it off.

The teamsters started it by halting all deliveries of gasoline, food, vegetables, coal, wood, and other necessities. They blockaded all of San Francisco by setting up picket lines across all highways leading into it. Housewives rushed to the grocery stores and cleaned off the shelves.

With Bloody Thursday fresh in mind, and with public opinion swung their way, almost every union quickly walked out: streetcar workers, butchers, cleaners and dyers, boiler-makers, bartenders, waiters, hotel employees, taxi drivers . . . The city was paralyzed.

Few automobiles were seen on the streets; the motorists had to conserve gasoline for a quick getaway from the city if needed. No streetcars were running. Virtually all stores were closed. All theaters, night clubs, and barrooms were shut down. Toughs roamed the almost-deserted streets, pilferers lurked in the alleys. Martial law was declared around the waterfront. Guards with bayoneted rifles stood outside the National Guard Armory on Mission Street. Thousands of steel-helmeted troops were brought in to maintain law and order.

People huddled around radios, waiting for news flashes. The *Chronicle* printed a story that a Communist army was marching on San Francisco from the Northwest, and that it "planned the destruction of railroad and highway facilities to paralyze transportation and, later, communication... (and would make the city) a focal point in a Red struggle for revolution and control of government."

Many people fled the city.

At that time Furuseth lived in a little third-rate room out on Divisadero Street. He wanted to get to the union hall to encourage his men to remain calm and sane, but the streetcar workers and taxi drivers were out. So, although then 80 years old and not well, he walked nearly three miles to the Sailors' Union hall on the waterfront. He pleaded for moderation. The communist element booed him off the stage. The long walk and the emotional crisis put too great a strain on his tough old heart. He collapsed, and was carried to St. Luke's Hospital.

Thoroughly exhausted, he slept most of the time. One day, propped up in bed, he felt a presence in the room, but he was too weary to open his eyes. If he had, he would have seen, standing in the open doorway, the 14-year-old boy mentioned in the preface of this book.

Although the Communists had welcomed the redbaiting because it increased their credibility among the strikers, they started to bear the consequences.

The National Guard blocked both ends of the street on which the headquarters of the Marine Workers Industrial

THE ABRAHAM LINCOLN OF THE SEA

Union was located. Police moved in and arrested 75 persons who were in the hall, and then proceeded to smash everything in the place.

Carloads of "citizen vigilantes"—a new entity—drove up to suspected Communist premises, smashed the windows with bricks, then moved in. They beat up anyone they found, and left the place a shambles. The police would arrive immediately and arrest the men who had been beaten up.

But when the vigilantes came to the building at Civic Center that housed the Communist Party's headquarters and the offices of the *Western Worker*, they found it deserted. They smashed the furniture and fixtures, and destroyed stacks of Communist pamphlets.

Over 400 Communists and "sympathizers" were jailed. The police announced that the "extermination raids" would continue until every Communist had been jailed or driven from the city.

After three days of chaos, the desire to continue the general strike began to cool. The economic pressures had proved to be too severe, the disruptions too unsettling. The word was passed along. Teamsters returned to work, moving cargo to and from the docks. A few days later, the longshoremen voted to end the strike and to submit all disputes to arbitration.

Gradually, normal traffic returned to the streets, stores and theaters opened, restaurants began serving customers, trucks rumbled through the streets, and the city came alive again.

Also, the Communists moved back into their headquarters, glass was replaced in the windows, typewriters began clicking, and new literature came off the presses. The *Western Worker* resumed publication.

On July 24, Furuseth got out of the hospital and spoke before a meeting of the SUP. He criticized the longshoremen's return to work, and urged the seamen to continue the fight against the fink hall—that could *not* be arbitrated. The other unions conceded that labor was licked. "I do not think it is over," Furuseth insisted. "I know it is not over if you are men." He contended that the seamen should not return to work until the fink hall was done away with.

Once again, his remarks were met with wild applause. Someone wrote, "Man after man came forward and shook Andrew by the hand."

"Tear Gas" Plant, president of the Waterfront Employers' Union, said the shipowners couldn't negotiate with the sailors unless elections were held to determine who was the bona fide spokesman for the seamen. A contest between the Marine Workers Industrial Union and Furuseth's International Seamen's Union flared up. But by an overwhelming eight to one vote, the ISU was established as the official bargaining representative. So, one result of the strike was the rejuvenation of the ISU.

On July 29, the sailors held a mass meeting, and admitted International Longshoremen's Association leaders to explain their position. Harry Bridges stood up to speak.

Furuseth had probably not even heard of him before the 1934 strike, but he soon learned that Bridges represented two things he detested: longshoremen and radicalism.

Bridges said his men were ready to break, that they had had enough of the strike. "The shipowners have us backed up." He acknowledged that the seamen could have good reason to be angry that the longshoremen had made a unilateral decision to quit. "I don't know how you fellows are going to take this," he said. "It's going to be a tough pill to swallow." Then he made his pitch. "It will be terrible if we go back tomorrow and the sailors stay out . . . We must go back together . . . If the longshoremen go back and the sailors stay out that will break the unity of the whole thing. That is the best thing we have in our hands. *Unity!*"

"Unity?" Why the last thing Furuseth wanted was unity with the longshoremen. He believed in craft unions, and staked his whole career on keeping the seamen free of entangling alliances—especially with the longshoremen. Here was a chance to break away from the intercraft "unity" that he viewed with alarm and disgust.

When Bridges finished talking, Furuseth stood up to start a rambling speech, occasionally quoting Scriptures. He urged the men to restore the integrity and strength of the International Seamen's Union, to refuse to cooperate with the fink halls, and to go their own independent way. The seamen had not struck in sympathy with the longshoremen, he said, but had struck independently with their own demands. Just because as an act of "damned cowardice" the longshoremen were going to "crawl back" to work didn't mean they should. The sailors, he declared, now stood alone. "We will win where the longshoremen couldn't."

Then this 80-year-old man, just out of the hospital, rose to the occasion with a masterful appeal to the sailors' militancy and anger. He suggested an act of dramatic defiance that would "wake up everybody."

"What do you think my propostion is?" he said. "It is horrible and yet it is the most beautiful you can ever think of . . . We are going to build a fire. Alongside of that fire we will have a can of petroleum, and each man who has got a fink hall book will come along there and he will dip it into that petroleum and throw it on the fire . . . The newspapers will know about it. The Associated Press will know all about it. The pictures will be shown all across the country."

With one grand stroke, Furuseth fired up the seamen's imagination, rescued them from their second-class position in the recent events, and seized the initiative from Bridges.

At 12:00 noon on the next day, the seamen gathered in a vacant lot near the Sailors' Union hall. They built a bonfire, and with cheer after cheer burned their hated fink books into a pile of ashes. A cross was erected to mark the grave of the fink hall. Despite his frail condition, Furuseth stood during the entire ceremony, contentedly smoking a cigar. He basked in the glow of yet another high point in his career ... not realizing it would be his last.

Fortified by the ritual, and after conciliatory gestures by the shipowners, the sailors returned to work. After 83 days, the Big Strike was over. The fink hall had been dealt a mortal blow, and was done away with.

During the strike, the Communists had been a convenient target for both government and business. Now that the strike was over, they claimed the strike had been entirely led by them. This was repeated so often that it was accepted by many as truth.

The Communists continued to disparage Furuseth, calling him vile names, trying to destroy the legendary "Abraham Lincoln of the Sea." They used all their means—pamphlets, leaflets, and word of mouth—in their attempt to lower the esteem in which he was held by the men.

Name calling didn't faze Furuseth, but he was concerned that the Communists were filling the heads of the young sailors with "radical" ideas. He wanted to fight back, but ... he was so tired ... so weary.

The story of Andrew Furuseth cannot be told without also telling about Harry Lundeberg.

He also was born in Norway, but 47 years after Furuseth. As a young man he went to sea and joined the Seattle branch of the SUP in 1923. Two days after the longshoremen's strike was called in 1934, he sailed into San Francisco as third mate on the steam schooner *James Griffith*. He walked off the ship and immediately returned to Seattle.

The 1934 Maritime Strike extended all along the West Coast. Seattle, too, was a battleground. It had its strikes, pickets, strikebreakers, and violence (Two men killed). There were police, tear gas, and attempts to "open the port." Here, too, it was charged that the strike was a Communist plot. Lundeberg took an active and militant part in the conflict.

After the strike, he was elected as the local patrolman (business agent). He also caught the eyes of some of the left wing leaders. Lundeberg "talked like a Wobbly," they said, although they thought he was "more or less apathetic" toward the Communist Party. A Communist-controlled newspaper in the Northwest hailed him as a "fighting progressive." When Harry Bridges came to Seattle, he admired Lundeberg's militancy, and called him a "fine trade unionist." In fact, Bridges was so impressed with Lundeberg that the following year he sponsored and promoted him for a high union position in San Francisco—an action that he would later regret. What Bridges didn't know was that Lundeberg *hated Communists.*

Both Furuseth and Lundeberg were born in Norway, sailed the seas for many years, and spoke with Norwegian accents. But in other respects they were as different as two people could be.

Furuseth always dressed in a business suit, rumpled though it might be, complete with a tie. Lundeberg was usually garbed in black dungarees, an open shirt, and a flat gray cap which he wore indoors and out.

Furuseth had an excellent command of the English language; he wrote letters and articles worthy of an English professor, and he could speak with ease before congressional committees or even with the president of the United States. Lundeberg's speech had its own kind of blunt eloquence, punctuated now and then with profanity.

Although they both hated Communism, Furuseth was so conservative that he began to deem as detested Communists not only members of the Party, but also anyone who disagreed with him. Lundeberg was a liberal, in tune with the Wobblies; although apparently never a member of the IWW, his thinking was similar to theirs.

Furuseth believed in accomplishing his goals by legislation and through court cases. But Lundeberg believed "an oldfashioned working over" brought more justice than a day in court. A big, brawny, intelligent man, he made it a point to systematically use violence as part of his arsenal. He participated in brawls himself, and bore battle scars proudly.

These two disparate men built up the union and made it prosper. Furuseth, literate and tenacious, freed the seamen from bondage and made them free men through the passage of the Seamen's Act. He caused their lives to be improved by additional legislation and by success in court cases. Andy Furuseth was what the seamen most needed . . . at that time.

But times had changed. New and different kinds of battles had to be fought. Lundeberg would emerge from the seaman's rank and rise rapidly to a high position of labor leadership. He, a dynamic representative of the new breed of union leaders, would become the virtual czar of the Sailors' Union of the Pacific. He would carry on the work that Furuseth had begun.

Chapter Twelve

Despite the publicity received by the Communists during the 1934 strike, its Marine Workers Industrial Union didn't fare well. This might have been partly due to the long campaign of police harassment—the many arrests, the raiding of its halls, and the vandalizing of its premises—but whatever the cause, it was the AFL seamen's unions that prospered as a result of the strike. Membership in the Sailors' Union of the Pacific shot up. The International Seamen's Union (still acting as agent for the SUP, the Marine Firemen, and the Marine Cooks and Stewards) won handily over the MWIU as bargaining agent.

In February 1935, the Communist Party ordered its members to infiltrate the Sailors' Union of the Pacific, with the objective of seizing control. The left continued to gain influence. Four months later, former members of the Communist MWIU were offically allowed to transfer to the SUP. Because of this, further tension developed between the conservative leaders of the International Seamen's Union and the left-leaning SUP.

Another aftermath of the 1934 strike was a growing acceptance of industrial unionism. The maritime unions had been successful in their common cause against the employers, and many of the union members felt they should preserve the alliance. Harry Bridges knew they weren't yet ready for the One Big Union, but he proposed an umbrella organization, a federation of the longshoremen, the sailors, and all other maritime unions.

Bridges called for a convention in Seattle on April 15, 1934, to form the Maritime Federation of the Pacific. He had been impressed with the relatively unknown sailor named Harry Lundeberg, and was successful in getting this "fighting progressive" elected as president. Since the headquarters of the new federation was to be in San Francisco, Lundeberg moved to that city and spent the rest of his life there as a union leader.

It didn't take long for Bridges to discover that Lundeberg was indeed a fighter, and that he also had a mind of his own. Lundeberg's main interest was concern for the sailors, not for the Federation. Bridges wanted centralized authority; Lundeberg wanted to protect the sailors' union's autonomy. He said, "We want the sailors to run the sailors' union, and the other maritime workers to run their unions. We don't butt into the internal affairs of other unions, and we don't propose to let other unions butt into our internal affairs."

The Communists were no longer happy with Lundeberg. The *Western Worker* denounced him as "individualistic," certainly a defamatory word in their vocabulary.

However, members of the Sailors' Union of the Pacific admired Lundeberg. He was a sailors' sailor, and was one of the new breed of union leaders whose thinking was in tune with theirs. In December 1935, they elected him secretary of the SUP (the office Furuseth had held for many years), and he resigned as president of the Maritime Federation.

Bridges and Lundeberg began a bitter and long lasting feud. Lundeberg referred to Bridges as "Needlenose" and "Fink." Bridges countered by calling Lundeberg "Old Melon Head." As one old-timer said, "They started squabbling with each other, and made a mess of it. Got to be quite a deal." He laughed, and added, "Lundeberg hired Bridges' secretary away from him."

When Lundeberg moved into SUP headquarters, he found a hard core of about 80 left-wingers in key positions. He hated Communists, calling them "psychos," "idealists who can't get on in the world," and "phony intellectuals plus a bunch of just plain lazy bastards." He said, "I wouldn't just knock one down. I'd kick him twice." He started to throw them out of the SUP.

At first, the Communists had tried to woo him, saying he was one of the chosen who, with the Party's build-up, could become the greatest union leader in the West. "Yah," Lundeberg said, "but I don't want to be a great union leader." That ended that.

On another occasion, he awoke one night in a hotel room, turned on the light switch, and saw three husky left-wingers at the foot of his bed. He yawned, stretched, and then slipped out a revolver from under his pillow. The intruders were lined up facing an open doorway and, one by one, were booted into the hallway.

In a waterfront battle with the left-wingers, his jaw was smashed by a blow with a lead pipe. Another time, someone fired shots through the windshield of his car; when the police tried to find out who the gunmen were, all Lundeberg would say was, "Sailors take care of their own problems."

In his own way, Lundeberg got rid of the Commies, although it took a few years to do it.

Furuseth's responsibilities as secretary of the Sailors' Union of the Pacific had been declining. Now, after 44 years of continuous service, the members had seen fit to elect someone else to take his place. Somewhat disappointed because he was no longer needed in San Francisco, he now spent even more of his time in Washington.

During the short periods in San Francisco, he had a room in the Norwegian Club at 99 Divisadero Street. The club gave him a taste, a slight feeling, of home—something he hadn't experienced since Bob La Follette died 13 years before. Every Thursday evening, fellow Norwegians gathered for a few drinks and then had dinner, which included singing, speeches, several skoals, and some lighthearted fun. (A tradition that is still carried on today.)

A few rooms on the third floor of the Norwegian Club were rented by bachelors. One evening, another roomer went into Furuseth's room to visit. He was surprised to see a revolver lying on the bureau with other objects Furuseth had emptied from his pockets. Furuseth never spoke of his personal affairs, and there was little use in asking. But he was apparently now in the habit of carrying a revolver with him. . . . Why?

In 1935, Secretary of Labor Frances Perkins appointed Furuseth as one of the American delegates to an important international conference in Geneva. He spoke long and often when he had the opportunity, but his views were shared by none of the other delegates, and he made no contribution to the meeting. The following year, someone else was selected as the delegate in his place. So, Furuseth suffered another disappointment: the knowledge that he was no longer needed —or wanted—in this capacity, either. His participation in international maritime affairs ended.

Out of respect for his past accomplishments, he was still appointed as a delegate to the AFL conventions. But most of the old-timers were no longer in attendance, and his views were outdated. He became a lonely figure who hung around the lobby rather than taking an active part on the convention floor. On the rare occasions when he did speak, he was as outspoken as ever, even knowing that his cause was hopeless and that the delegates would ignore what he said.

The Communists continued their campaign of character assassination.

Furuseth was a lonely man. He was tired . . . and ill.

All his life he had shunned personal publicity and acclaim. Only once did he seek recognition. A world-renowned sculptor, Jo Davidson, had made a statue of Senator Robert La Follette, which stood in the Statuary Hall of the Capitol in Washington. Years later, Furuseth consented to sit for Davidson, and was proud of the bust he created. Furuseth suggested that it should be placed in the headquarters of the SUP. Davidson agreed, but demanded that the sailors express their desire for the bust by contributing to a fund. After a few broad hints by Furuseth, without results, he laid the issue squarely before the officers.

"It would serve as a real information," he said, "as to what my real standing is amongst the men now. Do they really want me, or do they want to get rid of me? Have they some idea that my usefulness is over?"

No collection was ever made.

Feeble reasons were given, and Furuseth accepted the explanation without any show of emotion. But it pained him to know that the one and only time he requested some personal recognition, he had been turned down. He felt spurned, rejected—and with no way to pursue the matter without causing further humiliation.

But the hardest blow of all was yet to come.

Furuseth's closest confidant and lifelong friend in the labor movement was Paul Scharrenberg, who was born in

Germany in 1877 and who began shipping out in his teens. As a young man of 22, he had signed aboard the hell-ship *T. F. Oakes,* whose name had been changed to the *New York,* for a ten-months' voyage from New York to San Francisco—via Shanghai and Hong Kong. As the vessel approached the Golden Gate, she fell into bad weather and ran aground at Half Moon Bay. Scharrenberg swam ashore and ended up in San Francisco.

He applied for membership in the Sailors' Union of the Pacific. When he presented his discharge from the ill-reputed and ill-fated ship, Furuseth asked him the standard questions for applicants, and was so impressed with Scharrenberg that he later arranged to have him hired on as an officer in the union. Scharrenberg shared Furuseth's ideas on how a union should be run, and thought as Furuseth did. Perhaps for these reasons, the Communists turned their vitriolic rhetoric on him as they had on Furuseth. They called him "a fink," as well as "a traitor," and declared that "he is a scab and the son of a scab and the father of scabs. He is so scabby that he sweats pus."

Scharrenberg served the union well, and when Walter Macarthur resigned as editor of the *Seamen's Journal,* Paul Scharrenberg took his place.

But now, the new, militant leaders of the Sailors' Union of the Pacific intensified their rebellion against the old, conservative leaders. They vilified them verbally. They refused to follow orders of the executive board of the International Seamen's Union. In San Pedro, the SUP membership voted to ban the *Seamen's Journal*—now irreverently dubbed the "Seamen's Urinal"—from the union hall. Then they dropped a bombshell. They tried and *expelled* Paul Scharrenberg from the SUP!

Furuseth was furious, and he refused to accept the SUP expulsion of Scharrenberg because, in his words, "Andrew Furuseth takes no orders from the Communists."

Furuseth was convinced that the Communists had plotted the expulsion, and he included Harry Lundeberg in that category. It was true that Lundeberg was in rebellion against the old leadership, and he probably had a hand in forcing Scharrenberg out, but he was no "Communist."

One of the worst and saddest mistakes Furuseth made was to deem all "radicals" to be Communists; and as he grew older, he considered anyone who disagreed with him to be a radical. Whether because of senility or just Norwegian stubbornness, Furuseth was convinced that Lundeberg was a Communist, and nothing could change his mind. He didn't understand that Lundeberg hated Communists as much as he did; and further, that not only *could* Lundeberg do something about it, but that he *did*.

On the other hand, Lundeberg apparently understood Furuseth, because he admired and respected "The Old Man." He never spoke against him, despite the fact that Lundeberg's philosophy was liberal, while Furuseth was probably the most conservative and reactionary leader of any in the labor movement.

Furuseth and the other leaders of the International Seamen's Union demanded that Scharrenberg be reinstated; the SUP leaders refused. At an ISU convention, the delegates discussed the repeated violations by the SUP of the international executive board's orders, especially the refusal to reinstate Scharrenberg. There was even talk of revoking the SUP charter.

Presiding over the stormy convention proved too strenuous for Furuseth, and he was ordered by his doctor to remain

in his hotel room. After much reflection and anguish, Furuseth
sent a message to the delegates:

"It is with deep sorrow," he wrote, "but under absolute
conviction of necessity that I urge you all to vote unanimously
for expulsion."

The ISU revoked the SUP charter, thus expelling the
sailors from the ISU and the AFL.

With his strong paternal affection for the SUP, how
deeply this must have hurt Furuseth. What thoughts ran
through his mind as he sat alone in that hotel room? Did he
recall that day long ago when he, a young man, landed in San
Francisco? Did he remember the Coast Seamen's Union... the
conflict with the steamship sailors . . . how *he* started the
Sailors' Union of the Pacific... the years he spent with Bob La
Follette . . . the congressional hearings . . . the Seamen's Act?
He had battled the crimps, the longshoremen, the shipowners
. . . had given the SUP all he had . . . And now . . . he had to
urge that the charter be revoked... and his SUP be *kicked out*
of the ISU!

We don't know what Furuseth thought. All we know is
that his doctor said that the wound was so deep that he never
recovered. It was his death blow. And yet, his heart would not
quit. He lived another two years . . . often in hospitals and
nursing homes . . . always alone.

Chapter Thirteen

Harry Lundeberg carried on the work Furuseth had begun. But he had different problems, different solutions, and he handled them in a different way. Among other things, he faced bitter and confusing jurisidictional conflicts.

The new Congress of Industrial Organizations (the CIO) was organized, challenging the old American Federation of Labor. On the East and Gulf Coasts, a new union was formed, the National Maritime Union (NMU), representing 35,000 seamen. It affiliated with the CIO. On the West Coast, Harry Bridges took over the warehousemen, and converted his ILA into the International Longshoremen's and Warehousemen's Union (ILWU), which he also affiliated with the CIO.

So, there were now four rival major unions to contend with. On the East and Gulf Coasts, there was an AFL longshoremen's union and a CIO seamen's union; while on the Pacific Coast, there was a CIO longshoremen's union and an AFL seamen's union. A New Yorker article said that the situation was so complicated "that nobody can make head or tail of it . . . Everyone is at sea except the seamen."

As an example, the Sea Thrush sailed to the East Coast with a SUP crew, but returned to the West Coast with a NMU crew. When she arrived in San Francisco, Lundeberg declared her "hot," and put up a SUP picket line. In retaliation, Harry Bridges personally led his ILWU longshoremen through the SUP picket line. The two forces faced each other with swinging fists and bats. At least 25 or 30 men were knocked to the ground with cracked noses and bruised bodies.

Lundeberg fought these battles in his own way. The *Chronicle* reported that when the San Francisco police discovered a large cardboard box containing new 30-inch baseball bats in the rear of Lundeberg's car, he protested. "There were no bats in that car when we came down here . . . This is a Communist plot. Those bats were placed in the car after it was parked here." Years later, he admitted, "I had 50 ballbats in the tire compartment of my car . . . (A) cop saw them so I said it was a damn Communist plant to discredit loyal American sailors."

In Washington, Furuseth had lived for years in the attic of the old National Hotel on Pennsylvania Avenue, because of its central location. When the hotel burned down, he moved to the only other hotel where he could get cheap accommodations, the Hotel Ebbitt, a dilapidated building on a side street. After the ISU convention which revoked the SUP charter, Furuseth returned to his tiny bare room. Physically exhausted, he could do little but to sit and read. He did manage to continue his habit of writing letters—to President Roosevelt, among others.

Furuseth had never married, had no family . . . had no son. Every man seeks fulfillment, but sometime during his life he realizes he will fail in his quest. Regardless of what he has accomplished, there are things left undone. So, his hope lies in his son. Perhaps he will avoid the errors the father has made, will fill in the omissions, will succeed where the father has failed. Each man, generation after generation, has at least subconsciously been comforted by this thought. But... what if he had no son? What then? His own life loses some of its meaning. There is no one to carry on. His own death brings an end to hope.

Andy Furuseth had no son. Looking back in discouraged moments, his life could have appeared meaningless.

But he looked forward.

He took comfort in the white linen cloth.

Once he had been asked, "When you can no longer work, what provisions have you made for old age?" His answer was typical of the man. "When my work is finished, I hope to be finished. I have no provision for old age."

Two months after the ISU convention, he was taken to a hospital, and spent his remaining life either in a hospital or a nursing home. Paul Scharrenberg visited him frequently, telling him what was happening in the outside world, but sparing the old man any news about the death of the ISU.

One day, Scharrenberg was talking to Furuseth about monuments, and said, "Andy, you'll get a bigger monument than any of these other fellows."

Furuseth frowned. "Monument," he said. "I don't want a monument. When I'm dead, I want you to take my ashes, give them to someone, take them out as far from the shore as you can get, and dump them overboard ... as far from land as possible."

By September 1937, he was more dead than alive, and he was not allowed to see anyone.

He died on Saturday, January 22, 1938, in his 84th year.

His body lay in state in the auditorium of the Department of Labor building, the first time in the history of the Department that such a tribute had been paid to the memory of any person. The funeral was attended by Secretary of Labor

Frances Perkins, eight senators, eight congressmen, two Supreme Court justices, a Circuit Court judge, the minister of Norway, many union leaders, several businessmen and lawyers . . . and Jo Davidson, the sculptor.

His body was cremated and the ashes were taken to Savannah, where the urn was turned over to Thomas F. Webb, master of the merchant ship *Schoharie*. When the vessel was halfway between the shores of the United States and England—at latitude 47° 03' north, longitude 37° 12' west—the ship hove to and half-masted. After reading from the Bible, the skipper scattered the ashes on the sea—"as far from land as possible."

Paul Scharrenberg handled Furuseth's "estate." It consisted of less than 20 dollars in cash, his clothes, his Bible and a few other books, and the contents of his suitcase—his lifetime accumulation of material goods.

Officers of the American Federation of Labor, recalling the bitterness of Furuseth's fight in his last years, lamented, "All real seamen will ever regret that the last years of Andrew Furuseth's life were made miserable by the antics of the Communist element."

The SUP members must have felt a sadness at the 1936 split between "The Old Man" and the union, because after Furuseth's death the union commissioned a bust of him. It had failed to provide funds for the Davidson bust during Andy's lifetime, but hired a sculptor to create another one after his death.

The bust now stands in front of the SUP headquarters at 450 Harrison Street in San Francisco. The building is an impressive and fine example of the art deco "streamlined moderne" style, with the front portico resembling a ship's foredeck, and with columns resembling sails. The entrance is guarded by the busts of both Furuseth and Lundeberg; Furuseth's is on the right, and Lundeberg's on the left. The busts stand only about 75 feet apart, but, because of the outward curvature of the building, one bust is not visible to the other. And yet, both are turned at an inward angle so that Furuseth and Lundeberg appear to be staring at the same vision in the distance.

Furuseth had loved the sea, but stayed on land so he could devote his life to the freedom and welfare of the men before the mast. He had fought against crimps, shipowners, longshoremen, Wobblies, Communists, and others. He had fought them all.

Years before, as a young boy, he had stood alone in the middle of the road, and watched as his father, in horse and wagon, drew away. At the end, as an old man, he had watched as those who meant the most to him—his sailors—drew away from him. Once again, he had stood alone.

Was it worth it? He had gained nothing for himself, but his sense of fairness cried out for justice.

Would he do it again? Of course he would, because that is the way he was. He wrote at one time, "It seems that for forty years I have wasted my life, and yet if I had to go through it again I would act in the same way."

Was his life wasted? Of course not. Look back. Look back to recall how conditions were for the sailors when Furuseth first came on the scene. They led subhuman lives, were taken advantage of by the crimps, brutalized by the buckoes, and shunned by decent people. Almost all were single. How could a sailor get married? Gone for months at a time, never knowing in what port he would land next. And what mother would allow her daughter to be even seen with the proverbial "drunken sailor?" Even if he could find a girl who consented, there was no way a sailor could afford to support her. His wages were a pittance, and he never saw even that because the crimps and boardinghouse keepers usually got their hands on it first. He was always in debt, had no home, and perhaps at times did (understandably) drink too much.

And what are the conditions now? Today, able-bodied seamen earn over 2,400 dollars a month. Most are married and have homes of their own. Each sailor is entitled to a pension, and medical insurance for himself and his family. He can easily collect damages from his employer for any injuries incurred aboard ship.

In short, the sailor of today has an honorable vocation with decent pay, and he is no longer a victim of the crimps, of the boardinghouse keepers, or of the atrocities recorded in *The Red Record.*

And how did these changes come about? Because the sailor today is no longer a slave. He is living proof of the proclamation that "all men are created equal" with the "right to life, to liberty, and to the pursuit of happiness." Today, the sailor is a free man.

And no one did as much to gain this freedom than did Andrew Furuseth. He was indeed "The Abraham Lincoln of the Sea."

At times, he had, perhaps, been wrong in his beliefs and actions. He couldn't change with the times. He was stubborn. But all his forefathers had been Norwegians, people who had to suffer through months and months of cold, bitter winters, and who had to be stubborn in order to survive. He carried the genes of his ancestors. Furuseth was thoroughly Norwegian.

Perhaps he had lived too long. He reached the pinnacle of his career in 1915 with the enactment of the Seamen's Act, and he had completed his main life's work then. He was 61 at that time, and maybe should have retired, but he wouldn't—he couldn't—give up the fight. He believed sincerely in what he had said in his Labor Day speech at the University of California in 1927: "Work is worship—to labor is to pray, because it is to exercise the highest, the divine faculties implanted in us as the sons of God . . . Those that have been untrue have shared the fate of the tree without fruit. They have passed away because they encumbered the earth. Those that have been true have lived, and according to history and to religious belief, they are to live."

Furuseth had to do the work he believed in. He had to be "true," because those who are true "*are* to live."

There is something yet to come.

Tomorrow is also a day.